Environmental Educator Notebook

2nd edition, 2014
Edited By Jamie O'Donnell

Acknowledgements

The NOLS Environmental Educator Notebook was written by NOLS Field Staff. The primary authors and editors of this second edition are Jamie O'Donnell, MS, MAT, Adam Swisher, John Gookin, PhD, and Pat Kearney, MEd.

Other authors and contributors to this book include Darran Wells, MA, Andrew Weidmann, Marco Johnson, Bridget Lyons, Rob Maclean, Laura Schmonsees, Ron Reisberg, Ashley Graves Lanfer, Alexa Callison-Burch, Trevor Deighton, Jesse Burns, Marisol Sullivan, Garrett Hutson, PhD, Ryland Gardner, PhD, and Spencer Scheidt.

Special thanks to Rick Rochelle and Shannon Rochelle for their many years of work on the environmental studies curriculum at NOLS, which helped shape the overarching outcomes and themes for this edition.

The illustrations are by Alisha Bube, John Gookin, Jamie O'Donnell, and Jon Cox. Some images supplied by WikiCommons.

Note from the Editor

My own exploration of the natural world and process of learning about it has changed my life in many wonderful ways. The root of teaching students about the environment on a NOLS course lies in getting students excited to wonder about the world in which we live. Sharing our passion and appreciation for the places we travel is paramount to helping students connect to these places. The following curriculum is an attempt to provide a foundation of science, information, and ideas that might support you in teaching your own students. Most importantly, teach from your heart! Keep learning and exploring yourself, but never let a lack of knowledge steer you away from helping students ask questions. Our questions drive our learning and growth more than the answers we might provide. So observe, share readings, appreciate your surroundings, ask questions even when we know we won't know the answers, and help students explore all the amazing connections that exist in the natural world.

- Jamie O'Donnell
July 2013

Photos
Front cover: Kyle Duba
Back cover: Riley Hopeman

Published by
The National Outdoor Leadership School
284 Lincoln Street
Lander, WY 82520
www.nols.edu

ISBN-13: 978-1-882-045-03-7

CONTENTS
NOLS ENVIRONMENTAL EDUCATOR NOTEBOOK

CHAPTER ONE
ENVIRONMENTAL STUDIES AT NOLS
"All education is environmental education" - David Orr

Environmental studies is about human interaction with the environment. It includes life sciences, physical sciences, and social sciences, with a special interest in sustainable human systems. While the NOLS core values remain consistent through time, the curriculum we choose to emphasize and teach evolves. The environmental studies (ES) component of the NOLS curriculum serves as an example. As we learn more about the science of how the earth's biotic and abiotic systems function, and how we interact with those systems, our priorities for what we wish to impart to students on a NOLS course must change. We hope to empower our students as leaders in their own homes to enact their own environmental values.

Within the broader NOLS philosophy of education, environmental studies are a central theme that permeates nearly every class and activity, whether observing and studying ecological systems, exploring environmental ethics, applying leadership skills, pausing to enjoy beautiful scenery, or adapting your schedule to nature's rhythms. Environmental studies at NOLS are relevant, fun, and proactive. They are founded on the practical need to understand Earth's natural systems and how we interact as part of them. They are also inspirational as extended wilderness experiences that support development of a "sense of place" and an ethic grounded in deep appreciation for the natural world. A NOLS student is expected to go home with both the knowledge and desire to self-assess, implement change, and lead others as a responsible citizen and steward.

THE ENVIRONMENTAL STUDIES LEARNING OUTCOMES

The following environmental studies learning outcomes detail what we want our students to learn during their NOLS course. All outcomes must emphasize transfer of learning and prepare students to act as environmental leaders by assessing themselves, working towards sustainable changes in their own lives, and leading others toward a more sustainable future.

1) Students will explore **science**, with an emphasis on ecological relationships. Their exploration will reveal connections between living and nonliving systems, enrich their understanding and appreciation of place, and provide a knowledge base for making informed decisions both in the field and at home.

2) Students will develop a **sense of place** by experiencing wilderness and exploring their relationship with their surroundings.

3) Students will develop their own **environmental ethic** by exploring the natural world, studying ecology, and applying Leave No Trace principles.

4) Students will understand relevant **policy, land management, and environmental issues.** And, how scientific knowledge and ethics can guide decision-making for sustainable living.

5) Students will understand how they can **transfer** their learning to assess their own lives, make appropriate changes, and then lead others.

THE ENVIRONMENTAL STUDIES CURRICULUM MODEL

The model on the following page portrays how we strive to teach environmental studies at NOLS. Begin by teaching a foundation of science (abiotic, biotic, and the interaction of the two, emphasizing ecological concepts). Support students in developing a sense of place by running NOLS courses that inspire personal connections with the natural world. The combination of knowledge and appreciation helps students define their personal values and ethics. An exploration of land management and environmental issues allows students to synthesize their knowledge and ethics. Throughout the ES progression, strive for the transfer of ideas, concepts, and values to students' lives after NOLS. This helps students assess their own lives, make appropriate changes to live sustainably, and then lead others by sharing their passions, teaching others, and engaging as leaders in their communities.

EMPHASIZING ECOLOGY THROUGHOUT

As a new emphasis within science, we must more strategically address the ecological relationships that exist within our natural world. This helps better demonstrate to students the interconnectedness of living and non-living systems and provides a framework of knowledge for decision-making. Weaving the idea of ecology and interconnectedness throughout reinforces the idea that we are not visitors of the wilderness, or any other place for that matter. We are members of a web of life that has far-reaching impacts on living and non-living systems wherever we are. We breathe the air, use resources, produce waste and interact with other living organisms.

APPLYING SYSTEMS THEORY TO TEACHING ENVIRONMENTAL STUDIES

The study of ecosystems has revealed a complex web of interconnected systems, both living and non-living. Humans, and the decisions we make, are as much a part of ecosystems as any other living organism. As a result, social and economic systems overlap with ecological systems given that the decisions we make in these realms have consequences throughout. Reducing these complex systems to their "parts" as a means of studying them erodes the true nature of their interconnectedness. For this reason, the way we address environmental studies on a NOLS course should strive to interconnect the differing facets of the entire NOLS curriculum.

NOLS specializes in teaching leadership through wilderness experience. The extended time spent traveling through ecosystems provides an opportunity for students to experience nature and develop strong values and ethics regarding the natural world and how we live within it. We do our students a disservice if we neglect to connect their emerging environmental ethics with their emerging leadership skills. Many scientists now believe that we no longer have a significant gap in our understanding of ecological systems, but are nonetheless hindered by challenges in decision making. This implies that we may be falling into leadership pitfalls when it comes to addressing environmental issues. Knowing what to do may not be our limitation, but appropriately applying judgment in our decision-making may be the crux of the matter.

ENVIRONMENTAL STUDIES AT NOLS

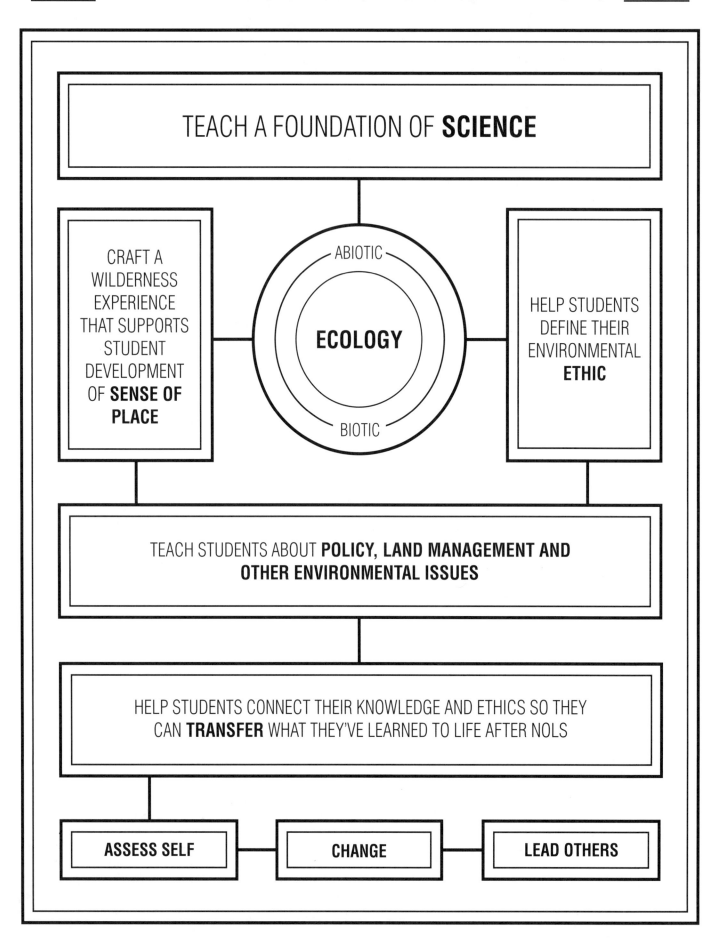

TEACH A FOUNDATION OF **SCIENCE**

CRAFT A WILDERNESS EXPERIENCE THAT SUPPORTS STUDENT DEVELOPMENT OF **SENSE OF PLACE**

ABIOTIC

ECOLOGY

BIOTIC

HELP STUDENTS DEFINE THEIR ENVIRONMENTAL **ETHIC**

TEACH STUDENTS ABOUT **POLICY, LAND MANAGEMENT AND OTHER ENVIRONMENTAL ISSUES**

HELP STUDENTS CONNECT THEIR KNOWLEDGE AND ETHICS SO THEY CAN **TRANSFER** WHAT THEY'VE LEARNED TO LIFE AFTER NOLS

ASSESS SELF

CHANGE

LEAD OTHERS

INTEGRATING ENVIRONMENTAL STUDIES CURRICULUM AND LEADERSHIP

As we learn and practice leadership, we must help students understand how they can assume the four leadership roles in addressing real-world environmental challenges. We must demonstrate the importance of the leadership skills in developing strong communities and teams that can make informed decisions. We can also thoughtfully integrate science as part of our competence. Effective decision-making rooted in scientific knowledge is as crucial in the frontcountry as it is with determining the best way to properly dispose of waste in the backcountry. As educators we ought to help students connect their personal journey and growth with their values and their environmental ethic. It will be through good leadership that our students enact their ethic, but we hope that the experiences they have on a NOLS course contribute to how they value the natural world.

HOW TO USE THIS NOTEBOOK

Each NOLS course evolves independently as a unique experience. The environments we visit, the participants, the conditions, and the instructors differ from course to course. Therefore, the activities, classes, and discussions that support learning outcomes on any given course will differ. Each I-team must individually define how they will approach environmental studies curriculum, and strive to clearly define how they will support student growth with respect to all five ES learning outcomes in the same way that we define a leadership progression to support our leadership outcomes. Our challenge is to clearly define what we hope to impart on our students, and focus our efforts toward those learning goals.

This instructor notebook is organized into seven chapters. The first chapter seeks to define the overall justification and framework for environmental studies at NOLS and to support instructor teams in creating a well-rounded ES progression. Each of the successive chapters addresses the five learning outcomes more specifically, provides theory and explanation for it, and includes a collection of activities and classes that instructors can implement in the field. As with all educational tools, instructors should meld these activities and classes to their own style and adapt them to the regions in which they work.

This collection of resources provides a foundation from which instructor teams can begin designing their ES curriculum. In lieu of teaching a linear progression, instructors are encouraged to creatively weave information from these classes and activities throughout the entire NOLS curriculum. For example, when teaching students how to dispose of waste properly in the backcountry, we can begin to weave in the ecological concept of nutrient cycles. Additionally, we can help students transfer this knowledge by discussing how we can dispose of waste in our homes through composting.

When approached effectively, numerous outcomes can be met through one activity. With a little creativity you could touch all five outcomes in one glaciology class (sense of place by learning more about specifics of that place, science by discussing how glaciers will "change" and how those changes interact with other global systems, environmental issues through discussions of climate change and their impacts on the glaciers in that range, and ethics and transfer of learning by connecting our values and decisions back home to impact on glaciers and climate systems). See the Environmental Studies Curriculum Matrix on page 6.

ENVIRONMENTAL STUDIES PROGRESSIONS

WHY - Teaching about the environment, the ecology of the places we visit, wilderness and land management issues, and how we interact with the world through our own personal ethic is an important part of a NOLS course and an over arching learning outcome for our students.

WHAT - Develop your ES progression around supporting the five ES learning outcomes. Remember that any one class, activity or assignment might support multiple outcomes. Use the ES activity matrix to give you ideas.

WHEN - On a stand-alone course choose times when students are comfortable, focused, and views are aesthetic. For semesters, think about what sections you will have and how they might naturally cater to particular outcomes or activities. For instance, canyons and river sections are great sections for land management classes and discussions as you travel through multiple-agency lands. Local issues can serve as visible examples of land management challenges. Winter sections are great for inspiring observation skills like tracking. You can also introduce the ecological concept of change by exploring how animals and plants are adapted to winter environments. Connect the ES curriculum to leadership by helping students realize that their knowledge and personal experience from this course influence their own perspectives and decision making after the course.

HOW - There are many ways to engage students in meaningful environmental studies. You must find ways that work for you and your instructor teams. Make sure that if you provide assignments like journal entries that you have a reason for them, and instructors participate. Revisit assignments through discussion. And, remember to teach better, not more. The following are some ideas for activities:

- A meaningful poop class that connects how we dispose of waste to ecology and reflects on a few of the ecological concepts like interconnectedness and cycles (nitrogen cycle). Connect this information to how we can dispose of organic waste at home by composting organic matter and sometimes even solid waste. Many people are using composting toilets at their homes.
- Have students teach a class on an environmental topic. This is a great way to get in ES curriculum. Provide them with topics and materials that will benefit the whole course and relevant to the course area. Teach them how to plan and teach a thoughtful and interactive class so they are set up for success, and provide feedback for the class. This supports the LNT Master requirements and provides real leadership/teaching learning opportunities.
- Journal prompts can be an effective way to get students thinking. Make sure instructors are active in this process. Use class time for structured journaling and then have students read what they wrote. If they know they're reading their writing, they are likely to put more effort into it.
- Have open-ended discussions on environmental issues like water, resources, gas and oil developments, and environmental ethics.
- Facilitate an environmental ethics class and have students define their own environmental ethic. What will this ethic look like in 20 years in practice?
- Challenge students to explore what strategies they can implement to reduce their ecological footprints, emphasizing positive change.
- Challenge students to explore how they can influence other people and the world around them to live more sustainably. This is where the LNT action plan can fit in.

ENVIRONMENTAL STUDIES CURRICULUM MATRIX

OUTCOME	CURRICULUM	ASSESSMENT

Science	**Classes**
	• Ecology based classes
	  – Poop class with soil ecology
	  – Ecological concepts part I&II
	  – Change class with time line activity
	  – Natural selection (adaptations)
	  – Ecosystem services
	• Science: Geology, botany, tracking, astronomy, climate, weather, glaciology, oceanography, local animals, etc. Make the topic relevant by weaving in ecological concepts to each.
	Activities
	• Ecological mapping activity
	• Readings
	• Nuggets—local issues, nitrogen fixers (cycles)
		• "Nuggets" – Connect them to concepts of ecology (Why is this thing where it is? What role does it play within the ecosystem?)
		• Ecological mapping activity that challenges students to map what they see and what is happening in the ecosystem capturing concepts of ecology.
		• Ecology quiz game (More for fun and additional learning)
		• Observation/field journals

Sense of Place	**Classes** • All natural history classes help students develop sense of place • Human history – these can often capture concepts of ecology **Activities** • Journal activities – writing/illustration • Silent hikes/Readings/Help them appreciate wildness • Structured reflection time	• Journal exercises • Illustrations • Poetry • Observation journals
Ethics	**Classes** • Environmental Ethics • LNT curriculum **Activities** • Discussions about how to teach/share LNT and other environmental ethics with others back home. • Challenge students to understand that some of our methods for minimizing impact in the backcountry result in impact somewhere else	• Journal entries defining environmental values & ethics • Camp sweeps • Student brainstorm sessions exploring why LNT is important • Student feedback sessions reflecting on how well groups are at minimizing their impact
Policy, Management & Environmental Issues	**Classes** • Land Management class • Ecological Footprint class **Activities** • Articles/readings – can be used as discussion prompts • Book reviews (semesters) • Discussions or debates on local and global environmental issues	• Journal assignment addressing how to reduce ecological footprint • Environmental Issue Nuggets • Book review to group • Facilitated discussions where everyone must contribute
Transfer of Learning	Every class, activity, discussion and assignment should attempt to help students transfer an idea, skill, or concept to their lives after NOLS. The ES outcomes should also be woven throughout the NOLS curriculum, not as a separate piece. **Activities** • A discussion at the end of the course that addresses how students can transfer their knowledge and experiences • Assess self – Change self – Lead others	• You can assess whether students speak about transfer, and research says the ethics generally transfer, but you categorically cannot assess transfer until it happens post-course.

The Environmental Studies Curriculum Matrix is a tool designed to help define a progression for environmental studies on a NOLS course, and provide an aid for assessing student outcomes. The matrix takes each of the five learning outcomes and breaks them down into potential classes and activities, and speaks to how best to assess for comprehension. The matrix is intended as a jumping-off point for ES curriculum.

• Teach science and natural history classes that emphasize the six ecological concepts and make them relevant to decision making. A weather class is a great segue to climate change and environmental ethics.

• Observation journals are great if well framed, role-modeled and students are provided with clear expectations. Provide time for students to do this in meaningful places. Do one yourself to demonstrate that it is meaningful enough that you are engaged as well. If you don't like it then they probably won't either.

• Have students do readings in the evenings and pass around some readings you can then discuss. Sometimes I share particular readings with just some students and then find others want to read them as well to be included.

- Take advantage of place-based teaching opportunities and teachable moments along the trail. "Hey check out this flower! This lupine is a nitrogen fixer and plays an important role in this ecosystem. We can grow plants like these in our own gardens to enrich the soil with nitrogen!"
- Have students choose a book with an environmental theme, read it, and then present what they learned or how it influenced them. Have them inspire a discussion. If you don't revisit what they have done by reading the book, the activity will likely loose meaning and students may wonder why they were asked to read it.

WHO - It is the responsibility of every I-team member from every section to contribute to the ES progression. This responsibility does not fall solely on any one instructor, semester section, or the proctor of a semester. Proctors and program supervisors need to ask other instructors to help define the ES curriculum for each section, and to teach classes. Climbing sections can use morning or evening sessions to discuss local environmental issues like water rights in Las Vegas Nevada, or grazing issues at Split Rock Wyoming. Don't allow challenges of balancing technical curriculum and risk management to rob students of a rich environmental studies curriculum.

STAND-ALONE COURSE ENVIRONMENTAL STUDIES PROGRESSION

Briefing
I-teams should briefly decide what curriculum they'll use to address each of the five learning outcomes. Remember, classes are only one tool. Discussions, coaching, teachable moments, activities, journal assignments, and structured reflection/observation time are all vehicles through which these outcomes might be reached. Consider beforehand how you'll assess the ES curriculum. Every NOLS course is different as is every NOLS experience. This is not a class list, just one path towards touching all five learning outcomes that may serve as an example. We all know the realities on course that impede our ability to cover curriculum. Be creative in finding ways to weave environmental studies throughout your course without it overwhelming your schedule.

Orientation
Define basic expectations for the ES curriculum along with other curriculum (if they expect it, they will be prepared for it). You should have decided what, if any, assignments students must complete. Tell students that you'll emphasize ecology and natural science, sense of place, ethics, environmental issues (Policy and Management), and how each of these transfers to their lives back home.

First Two Days
Teach a poop class that relates decisions on where and how to dispose of waste to ecosystem functions (review the class, use the terminology!) Through this, you can conceivably introduce the ecological concept of cycles, interconnectedness and energy flow.

First Week
Introduction to the LNT principles and the idea of LNT as an ethic. Connect the principles to the ecology that drives how we minimize our impact.

Decide how you'll address the six concepts (Scale, interconnectedness, energy flow, cycles, change, and dynamic balance) in an introductory ecology class.
- Maybe you only teach three concepts (Ecological concepts part I – scale, interconnectedness, energy flow), or teach one each day.

- The "Change Class with Geologic Time line Activity" is a good follow-up to ecological concepts part I and addresses the ecological concepts of change and dynamic balance quite well.
- A nature nugget on a local plant that is a nitrogen fixer is a great vehicle for covering the ecological concept of cycles (the nitrogen cycle).
- These concepts can easily be taught through other natural history classes as well. Try to make them relevant in your environment and to students' lives. Once you've taught them, you can easily refer to them in discussions and through teachable moments.

By the End of Week Two
Provide some structured reflection time. You may choose to provide a writing or observation prompt, or you may let them use it however they choose.

Consider what natural history class might best connect people with the environment you are in and teach that or truncate it into a trail side teachable moment that each instructor agrees to cover on the trail. (Weather, glaciology, tracking, a class introducing a local issue)

By the End of Week Three
Present an environmental ethics class/discussion with a follow-up assignment where students define their environmental values and their plan for enacting them in the future as an ethic.

A land management or environmental issue class can emphasize ecosystem services and the notion that how we manage land—or attempt to solve some issue—impacts the services our ecosystems can provide humans (clean air, clean water, habitat, biodiversity, pollinators, etc.).

Discuss ecological footprints. Connect this to land management since many of the resources we need come from our public lands.

Last Night in the Field
Help students reflect on the course and connect learning to their lives back home.
- They have learned to live well with very little.
- They have considered their values and how to enact them back home through their ethic.
- They must apply leadership to influence positive change.
- Sharing their passion for the outdoors and the environment with others.

SEMESTER ENVIRONMENTAL STUDIES PROGRESSION

A semester ES progression is very similar to a stand-alone course progression. On a semester course we simply revisit concepts throughout all the sections and develop them further. This likely means we do follow-up ecology classes, and include additional activities and assignments challenging students towards inquiry, observation, and reflection while in the field. We should provide more specific environmental issues and examples from locations we visit. Be cautious not to assume that environmental studies will happen on another section. The following list could supplement what happens on a typical stand-alone course:
- Ecology (part II) – choose one of the additional ecology classes that develops a principle in greater depth (Natural selection class, ecosystem services class, change class with time line activity, ecosystem mapping activity).
- Ecological footprint class– a great class to extend the environmental ethics class as it combines the reality of what we consume with our ethics.

- Revisit LNT each section and differentiate how different physical factors influence ecological processes and consequently how we choose to minimize our impact.
- Additional and appropriate natural history classes (weather, astronomy, glaciology, animal tracking, speleobiology, marine ecology, botany, etc.) that educate students on these environments and help build their sense of place. Strive to connect these to the six concepts of ecology and make these relevant to life after NOLS.
- Additional structured reflection time, silent hikes, solos.
- Collection of readings for students.
- Possible environmental/ecology book to be read on one section.
- Opportunity to teach an environmental topic (nature nugget).

ASSESSING STUDENTS ON ENVIRONMENTAL STUDIES
By Jamie O'Donnell and Pat Kearney

When compared to other curriculum areas, environmental studies can be challenging to assess. Most of the leadership skills, outdoor skills, and technical skills can be practiced throughout a NOLS course, and instructors have opportunities to see and quantify students' progress. Environmental studies curriculum must be creatively designed with assessment in mind from the beginning. If not, you may find yourself on the last night of your course trying to decide how to assess students on ES while writing evaluations. Given the assessment challenges, we must strive to structure curriculum that engages students and helps them demonstrate their understanding, so that we can fairly assess their learning.

- *Why do we assess?* We assess to help the learner understand some things about their understanding on various topics as well as to evaluate our ability to teach and transfer knowledge/information.
- *Who is doing the assessment?* The instructors, the student, both, peers, an external audience etc.?
- *When is the assessment done?* During, on-going, upon completion or much later (ethics)?

Using a Rubric
A rubric is a structured tool that helps instructors determine learning outcomes, consider curriculum flow, and provides objective metrics to evaluate student performance. Consider a rubric for ES assignments or the entire ES curriculum that evaluates students on three components: the content, the process, and the product. Content knowledge evaluates the extent to which students understand the material. Process evaluates how much energy, research, thought, and care the learner put into acquiring new knowledge or in creating the final product. Finally, evaluate the product itself (paper, class, nature nugget, journal entry, etc.).

Students can use a rubric as a way to self-assess during the project and instructors can use it as a way to gauge curriculum progress and student performance. Grades can be distinguished by any combination of the three categories, or as an average of them all. For example, instructors could evaluate students as receiving a "B" in content, an "A" in process and a "C" in product and choose to leave them separate or average them together (a "B"). It is important that students are aware of how, if at all, the rubric will be weighted and/or distinguished.

Ideally rubrics are designed before the assignment(s) and with curriculum progressions in mind to support the learning outcomes highlighted on the rubric. In addition, rubrics ought to be provided to the students so the project structure and expectations are very clear to the learner and instructors. The questions above (why, who and when) should be answered during the rubric creation process.

Please see the next page for an example rubric designed for a potential student project using this instructor notebook. Rubrics are intended to be introduced at the beginning of a course and followed up with detailed coaching by the instructors.

Additional Thoughts for Assessing ES Curriculum
While planning curriculum progressions, identify how you can address each of the five ES learning outcomes. Remember, creatively planned activities and classes can address multiple outcomes.

Once you have decided what you'll teach, consider how you'll assess student learning prior to leaving for the field. Assessment ideas include:
- **Reflections** through journal entries. These can be prompts you provide—like a five minute post-class writing exercise—where students reflect on how they can transfer knowledge, or reflect on what the knowledge means to them. Consider creating a forum for students to share what they write, making their thought process/learning public to you and other students.
- **Observation journals** where students conduct a series of entries about the environment they explore throughout their course.
- **Student taught classes and nuggets**. Provide a clear structure for students on what will be evaluated and provide them with tools to teach successfully.

Consider what resources you need to allow students adequate access to information and make them easily available. Role model learning and scientific inquiry to your students. Make a point to visibly use some of the course resources to research aspects of your course area. Engage students in that process.

Assessment can be used as an additional learning opportunity for you and your students. Design reflections or assignments so that they can be shared within the group. This lends a greater sense of accountability to students knowing they'll be sharing their product to the group. It also, demonstrates that you see value in that product for the group's learning and not just as an assignment you'll "grade" them on.

GRADING RUBRIC

Point System	Content	Process	Product
A — Exceptional (+)	• Used knowledge and terminology to demonstrate an understanding of subject-specific content and concepts, appropriate to the age level, using descriptions, explanations, and examples (e.g., these specific trees and plants tend to grow on north facing slopes). • Understands and is fluent with the scientific inquiry and ecological concepts.	• Formulated a clear and focused research question and used the scientific inquiry to investigate (e.g., why is there more vegetation on north facing slopes?) • Used methods accurately to collect and record information consistent with the research question, effectively addressed the research question.	• Final product (nature nugget, mini-class, or journal entry) is well delivered, creative, clear, and engaging to the audience. • Final product clearly demonstrates the use of and fluency with scientific inquiry • Final product clearly connects learning to one (or multiple) ecological concept, or illustrates how their research question was not related to an ecological concept.
B — Meeting Expectations (√+)	• Demonstrated some new knowledge of new content and concepts with limited description, examples, or explanations. • Demonstrated an understanding of both scientific inquiry and ecological concepts.	• Research question and use of scientific inquiry met expectations. • Methods used were accurate, met expectations and produced some data.	• Final product was well delivered and clear. • Use of scientific inquiry met expectations. • Connection to ecological concept meet expectations.
C — Meeting Basic Requirements (√)	• Demonstrated limited new knowledge of new content and concepts. • Demonstrated limited fluency with scientific inquiry and/or ecological concepts.	• Formulated research question was vague and poorly thought-out, and did not fully use scientific inquiry . • Limited methods or techniques were used to research question yielding little data.	• Final product was disorganized, hard to follow, and was challenging for audience to engage with. • Final product did not fully reveal use of scientific inquiry. • Product did not clearly connect to an ecological concept, or was inappropriate to the content.
D — Minimal or No Progress (Δ)	• Incomplete or not submitted.	• Incomplete or not submitted.	• Incomplete, not submitted, or unsatisfactory.

Grading students on environmental studies outcomes can often prove to be a difficult and arbitrary task. This grading rubric provides some clarity to help differentiate between letter grades. In order to properly assess for environmental studies, it is important to set up expectations early in the course, and follow through with the intended curriculum. Try to avoid blanket grading a student group because they weren't set up for individual assessment.

CHAPTER TWO
SCIENCE: ABIOTIC, BIOTIC, AND ECOLOGY

WHY WE TEACH SCIENCE

Science, from the Latin *scientia*, meaning "knowledge," is how humans further our understanding of the natural world through exploration and research. The scientific method is a process of generating predictions (hypotheses), collecting evidence through observation, testing hypotheses, and then drawing conclusions. This process seeks to provide the best possible explanation for a natural phenomenon. Scientists use peer review to monitor how well the scientific method was used, before each study gets published. Explanations change as we gather more information and refine our predictions and conclusions. Science never achieves absolute truth, but it does provide us with theories like gravity and evolution that are accepted by experts in various scientific fields.

Observation

While practicing science in the pure sense is unrealistic on a NOLS course, observation remains a vital component of exploring wilderness and ecosystems. Observation expands our connection with these places and provides a vehicle for exploring why things are they way they are. In addition to making observations, we supplement learning with other scientific knowledge about natural history and ecosystem function to foster an appreciation and understanding of place. This broadened knowledge serves to inform our decisions regarding how we choose to interact with our environment on our course and once we return to our homes.

Values

Scientific knowledge alone does not solve our numerous land management and environmental challenges. Values–our chosen behaviors and priorities—influence the outcome of these challenges. Science provides us with knowledge that contributes to how we interact with living and nonliving systems, as with our Leave No Trace (LNT) principles, but our values determine the extent to which we employ any particular knowledge. A wilderness journey rooted in experience, with opportunities to learn about places and the processes that shape those places, is an important mode for developing connections to the natural world and influencing our values.

Teaching Science

Teaching science classes in unfamiliar course areas can be challenging, but you can always teach students the ecological concepts then guide them to study the natural world as a scientist would. Students who learn to ask their own questions are more engaged, take greater ownership of their learning and learn more. An instructor modeling inquiry can be a powerful tool in helping students learn how to learn.

Ecology is the foundation for environmental studies at NOLS. It is the rationale for LNT practices. It helps us understand our place in the global biome. It helps us connect across the curriculum so students sometimes learn risk management and environmental studies at the same time. You should read, "Teaching the Six Ecological Concepts" first. With this background educators can connect curriculum to a foundation and reference key concepts to future classes. Teaching the six concepts to students first can provide a way for students to more easily understand each subsequent class.

SCIENCE INQUIRY

Science inquiry is a teaching method that draws from the process scientists use to answer questions about the natural world. It helps people informally apply the scientific method to everyday curiosities. This is the same experiential learning method we use elsewhere at NOLS, but it has tighter controls to help streamline the experimental process. It is simple to include science inquiry on any NOLS course, but it is especially important that students understand the process on semester courses where students earn college or high school biology credit.

Scientists generate predictions (hypotheses), collect evidence through observation, test these predictions, and then draw conclusions. Science inquiry applies this method to educational settings by challenging students to ask questions, make observations, and then draw conclusions based off those interactions. The National Science Teacher's Association claims that "scientific inquiry... is at the heart of how students learn. From a very early age, children interact with their environment, ask questions, and seek ways to answer those questions. Understanding science content is significantly enhanced when ideas are anchored to inquiry experiences." (National Science Teachers Association position statement on Science Inquiry: http://www.nsta.org/about/positions/inquiry.aspx).

Science inquiry can enhance student learning experiences and help them understand the process that scientists use to answer questions about the natural world. At NOLS we use numerous modes of teaching environmental studies, so not every learning opportunity will be well suited to science inquiry. When it seems beneficial to desired learning outcomes, this method should be used, but don't force it. The following list of ideas can help you integrate science inquiry into the courses you teach.

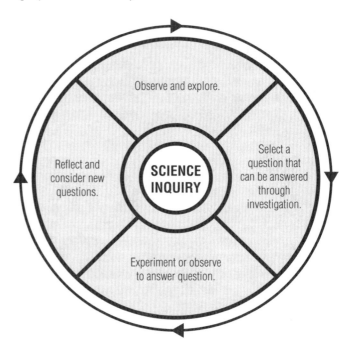

The process of Science Inquiry follows a continuum of observation, investigation, experimentation, and reflection. The continuum can be applied to all aspects of life, and is a powerful tool for critical thinking.

ENVIRONMENTAL EXPLORER – USING SCIENCE INQUIRY ON NOLS COURSES

Science inquiry is a teaching method that draws from the process scientists use to answer questions about the natural world (Scientific Method). Scientists generate predictions (hypotheses), collect evidence through observation, test these predictions, and then draw conclusions. Science inquiry challenges students to ask questions, make observations, and then draw conclusions based off those interactions.

Learning Objectives - The Learner Will be Able to:
- Make observations that lead to curiosity and questions
- Craft a question based off curiosity that can be answered/explored through further investigation and observation.

Class Outline
Briefly teach the scientific method and share its benefits as a tool for answering questions. The scientific method is as follows:
- Generate predictions (hypotheses) for unanswered questions.
- Collect evidence through observation that allows you to test the validity of your hypothesis.
- Draw conclusions – your observations/data should support your hypothesis.

Provide examples of how we can use this method to problem solve in our daily lives:
- My whisperlite isn't working properly. "Why isn't it working properly?"
- Hypothesis: "I think the pump is NOT pressurizing the fuel bottle."
- Experiment: Unscrew the fuel bottle to test whether air leaks out indicating whether it's actually pressurized.
- If it is pressurized, create another hypothesis to test and narrow down the problems.
- Change only one variable at a time in your testing so that, in the end, you can identify specifically what the problem is.

Explain that science inquiry uses the same process as the scientific method to explore your surroundings. Set expectations for students and how they will ask a question about their surroundings and then make observations in an attempt to answer their question. The emphasis of this activity is to help students notice what is around them, not to look up information in a book.
- Ask students to make observations about their surroundings during the first week of the course. Challenge them to focus on their curiosity and to generate questions they have based off what they see around them. This is the hard part.
- With your help and support, get them to identify one question that they can answer or come closer to answering through further observation or simple experimentation.
- Provide structure to their observations and have students make notes, draw pictures, and write down observations that help them answer their questions.
- Set a time when students will all briefly present their questions to the group and then later have them briefly present the conclusions they drew as well as new questions they have as a result of their inquiry.

Topics for Teaching Science Inquiry
Stove Cleaning
- Make observations about how your stove is not performing.
- Predict what part of your stove is malfunctioning or requires cleaning.

- Change just one variable by fixing or cleaning what you predicted is problematic.
- Draw conclusions about whether your predictions were correct.
- If the conclusions weren't correct, come up with a new prediction and repeat the process.

Weather
- Spend a few days observing weather patterns (winds, temperature, storms, etc.).
- Based on your observations, come up with a question that interests you:
  - Do the winds usually flow up canyon in the mornings and down canyons in the afternoon?
  - Is the coldest part of the night, truly just after the sun hits an area?
  - Is there a correlation between temperature and storm activity?
- Then come up with a way to make some observations that will help you draw conclusions.
- Record your observations through notes, drawings, etc.
- Draw conclusions and determine whether what you thought would happen or not.
- Based off what you concluded, what new questions do your observations generate?

Lake and Stream Ecosystems
- Have students poke around in a stream or lake and observe what they see. Ask them whether they are seeing different organisms in different places with different habitat types.
- Have them come up with a question about certain organisms or characteristics related to these ecosystems.
  - When are algae present in streams (upper streams, lower streams, big small, lot's of sunlight, less light)?
  - Are there more organisms in fast running water or slow water?
- Then have students make some observations that help them draw conclusions.
- Based off what you concluded, what new questions do your observations generate?

Birds
- After doing some basic observing of birds, have students come up with some questions.
  - Where am I seeing certain species of birds?
  - Do some species always land high in trees, low in trees, on the ground, in shrubs?
  - At what time in the morning do I first here a particular species of bird start singing?
- Then have students make some observations that help them draw conclusions.
- Based off what you concluded, what new questions do your observations generate?

Plant Adaptations
- Teach a basic plant adaptations class.
- Allow students to walk around and look for examples of adaptations from the environment in which you are traveling.
- Have students come up with questions about how the adaptations they see vary from species to species or plant to plant as each plant's microhabitat changes.
  - Do individuals in a slightly drier area have more elaborate manifestations of a particular adaptation to help them survive, or are they just smaller less healthy individuals?
  - Do all individuals of the same species have all the same adaptations or do some have ones that others lack?

- Then have students make some observations that help them draw conclusions.
- Based off what you concluded, what new questions do your observations generate?

Habitat
- Have students make some basic observations about the habitat that a particular plant or animal occupies.
- Then have them come up with some questions related to that relationship.
  - Does that flower only live on dry slopes, or does it also live in moist meadows?
  - Do I see that squirrel in pine and spruce forests?
  - How often do I see those two plants together?
- Then have students make some observations that help them draw conclusions.
- Based off what you concluded, what new questions do your observations generate?

Scale
- Make some basic observations about the ecological scale at which species occupy a landscape.
- Come up with questions about ecological scale.
  - How does scale influence species diversity? ($1m^2$, $100 \ m^2$, $1000 \ m^2$) Is it high at one scale but proportionally lower at another measured by species per square meter?
- Then have students make some observations that help them draw conclusions.
- Based off what you concluded, what new questions do your observations generate?

Other Potential Topics
- Behavior – what do those critters spend their time doing?
- In what ways does elevation influence the distribution of life?
- In what ways does aspect influence the distribution of life?
- Interactions – are their interactions between certain species of organisms in this environment?
- Correlations – can I identify relationships between certain terrain, rock types, or formations, with other variables like water movement, weather, organisms, etc.?
- Adaptations – do local organisms have common themes for adapting to the local environment?

Fun Twists
- Have students come to their meeting to present their findings dressed in a costume that is related to their question.
- Establish the meeting as a cocktail party where students must mingle and try to answer each other's questions.

Conclusion and Transfer of Learning
- Once everyone has presented their findings, highlight the value of inquiry both as a tool for answering questions about the world, but also for connecting to the places we call home.
- Check for understanding by asking students what the steps are in the inquiry process.
- Ask students if they have any questions about their home environments based off what they have learned about this local environment.

THE SIX ECOLOGICAL CONCEPTS

Ecosystems are complex systems where interconnectedness is the predominate form of organization. They are composed of both living and non-living parts. Ecology is the scientific study of interactions that determine the distribution and abundance of organisms within this network. To fully understand the complexity of life we must first recognize some basic principles about life:

1) Life exists as an interconnected web.
2) Matter cycles through this web.
3) The sun's energy drives these cycles that ultimately support life.

Understanding these three principles reveals the significant ties humans have to ecological processes. Processes we rely on for a variety of ecosystem services that include: clean air, clean water, healthy soil, pollination, and to transform organic waste into fertile soil. From these basic principles we can further identify six important concepts in ecology that more specifically define how ecosystems function, interact, and change through time: **scale, interconnectedness, energy flow, cycles, change**, and **dynamic balance**. These six concepts should guide and extend our environmental studies curriculum on a NOLS course. If we understand the basic concepts of ecology and how they define patterns and processes in ecosystems, we can apply them in our own lives to guide decision-making and solve many ecological problems we face. (Capra in Ecological Literacy p.20)

Systems Theory
The study of ecology demonstrates the interconnectedness amongst species and between species and their physical environment. What happens in one part of a system influences other parts of that system. We can apply this same "systems theory" when teaching ecological concepts on a NOLS course by connecting these concepts throughout our entire curriculum, as they too are interconnected. Understanding basic ecology helps guide our daily decision making regarding how we operate as individuals on planet earth. When we discuss decision making as part of a leadership progression, we could broaden the concept to other types of decisions that we will make throughout our lives related to resource use and ethics. Our students will participate as community members that lead others and we should remind them that they can assume all four leadership roles as environmental stewards, and do, whether they choose to or not.

Weaving in ecological concepts to strengthen and broaden a more specific topic or class is preferable to trying to teach the concepts independently and out of context. For example, when we teach pooping in the woods we should remind students of the ecology that helps guide our management of that impact on ecosystems. It is a great opportunity to reference the concepts of cycles, like the nitrogen cycle, and interconnectedness between the organisms and the soil and those in your poop. Risk management represents an opportunity to connect building judgment with future decision making related to sustainable choices that will impact future generations.

Ecosystem Functioning
The six ecological concepts we define in our curriculum shape ecosystems and allow us to understand how they function, interact and change through time. This understanding is crucial because healthy, functioning ecosystems provide us with goods and service necessary for our survival.

Sustainability in the ecological sense can be defined as, "the capacity for a given ecosystem service to persist at a given level for a long period of time." (Hooper et. al. 2005) In the social sense, sustainability is when, "communities are designed in such a manner that their ways of life, technology, and social institutions honor, support, and cooperate with nature's inherent ability to sustain life." (Capra xiii) The foundation of sustainability lies in understanding basic concepts of ecology and how they define ecosystem functioning. This knowledge can improve our decision-making that governs how we operate within our communities, which rely on healthy ecosystems.

.

> "*Ecosystem Functioning reflects the collective life activities of plants, animals, and microbes and the effects these activities – feeding, growing, moving, excreting waste, etc. – have on the physical conditions of their environment. A functioning ecosystem means one that exhibits biological and chemical activities characteristic for its type. A functioning forest ecosystem, for example, exhibits rates of plant production, carbon storage, and nutrient cycling that are characteristic of most forests. If the forest is converted to an agroecosystem, its functioning changes.*"
>
> (Naeem et. al. 1999).

The Six Concepts of Ecology

Using a framework created by Fritjof Capra, six major concepts of ecology can be defined:

1. Scale (nested systems)
2. Interconnectedness (networks)
3. Cycles
4. Energy flows
5. Change (development)
6. Dynamic balance.

These concepts all interact together and define how ecosystems function, or how nature sustains life. They can further be used to understand ecological sustainability.

1. Scale (Also called Nested Systems)

Life can be studied at different scales, and regardless of the scale investigated it operates like a network—each level can be "nested" into another. Together atoms form molecules, which form macromolecules (carbohydrates, lipids, proteins, and nucleic acids), macromolecules are the building blocks of cells. Cells nest together to form organs, which form organ systems, which together compose organisms. Organisms of the same species that interact together form populations. Populations of different species that interact form communities, and different communities that interact together in their environments form ecosystems. Ecosystems that interact form biomes and all the biomes on earth compose the biosphere. While the complexity of one level may be greater than another, the same basic pattern of organization exists at all levels. The answer to any particular question in nature may vary depending upon the scale at which that question is analyzed. A smaller group of humans at the population level may live sustainably while humans at the biosphere level appear to being using more resources than earth can sustain. While a field with a hundred varieties of corn is considered to have high genetic diversity at the population scale, it has low species diversity at the community scale.

> cell ⇒ tissue ⇒ organ ⇒ organ system ⇒ organism ⇒ population ⇒ community ⇒ ecosystem ⇒ biosphere

Ecosystems change over different time scales as well. Climate may change over periods of decades as a result of atmospheric changes or periods of millennium as a result of planet orbital shifts.

2. Interconnectedness (Also called Networks)

All living organisms not only interact continually, but also depend on each other in what is known as a network or web of life. Through this network, energy enters and flows. The energy drives cycles through which matter (air, water, nutrients) continually flows. Using the web of life as a model, we can begin to identify patterns of how living organisms interact and impact each other.

How Organisms Interact

Competition is a driving force in nature where individuals compete for limited resources. Competition within individuals of the same species is intraspecific competition. Those individuals in a population best adapted to their environment to compete for resources survive and reproduce (Fitness). Competition between different species is referred to as interspecific competition. It ensues when two or more species in a community occupy similar habitats and use similar resources, referred to as sharing a similar *niche*. When the niches of two species overlap considerably, the competitor better adapted to accessing resources will either displace the rival, or force the rival to occupy another niche. Competition, within a species or among different species, acts as a driving force that naturally selects those individuals best adapted to compete for limited resources. This selective process defines how populations evolve through time as environments continually change.

Predation occurs when an individual of one species (predator) eats an individual of another species (prey) to gain energy and results in the death of the prey. Predation acts as a pressure that selects those individuals best adapted for capturing prey and those prey best adapted to avoiding predators. In this way, evolving traits of predator and prey impact how the other evolves (co-evolution) in an arms race fashion.

Symbiosis defines any close and long-term relationships between two different species. These relationships can be mutually beneficial (mutualism), beneficial to one species while the other is unaffected (commensalism), and beneficial to one species at the expense of the other (parasitism). Symbiotic relationships also drive the evolutionary process; species will co-evolve and traits of one species drive changes in traits of the other species.

The Role of Biodiversity in the Web of Life

Given the complex nature of interactions between organisms within the web of life, diversity at all levels (genetic, species, and ecosystem) supports ecological resiliency. A network of species with overlapping functions can better sustain environmental change as one species can assume the role of another in its absence. The more diversity there is, the more overlap of function occurs, and consequently the better the network can sustain change. This concept is best demonstrated by two examples.

In the first example, a mono-crop of corn with little genetic diversity is very susceptible to environmental changes (disease, climate etc.) as its homogenous nature precludes it from surviving some pressure it is not adapted to. In a field with multiple varieties of corn, some environmental pressure might destroy some varieties, while other varieties possess adaptations to withstand the pressure.

In the second example, an ecosystem with many species is more resilient to change over one with few because the elimination of one species can be "absorbed" by other species with similar roles. If an ecosystem has only one grazer and that grazer goes extinct, the ecosystem will suffer a ripple effect of change as grazing ceases.

Species biodiversity is not consistent through geologic time (Biodiversity during of the Phanerozoic). The fossil record reveals five abrupt drops in species diversity (mass extinctions) that recovered slowly over millions of years. This is a natural part of a dynamic universe. However, most biologists agree that we are entering our 6th mass extinction as a result of human alterations to ecological processes and systems. While this change can be viewed as natural to earth's evolution, it will negatively impact humans directly given that we derive great benefit from biodiversity for numerous ecosystem services.

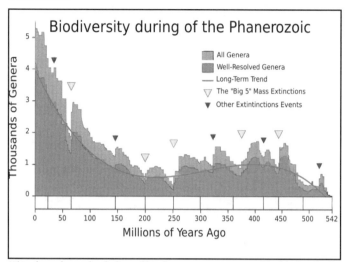

This chart shows the decline of biodiversity over time, and highlights the five most significant mass extinctions. It is currently thought that we are amidst the sixth great extinction due to a recent sharp decline in biodiversity.

Change in Population Size Through Time

Populations, like all things in nature, fluctuate through time as their ability to access resources changes or the survivorship in changing environments fluctuates. Populations grow when individuals access resources well, thereby increasing survivorship (more individuals survive than die during a given time period) and they shrink when competition reduces access to resources and survivorship is low (more individuals die than survive). Growth may be linear through time when a population increases a certain amount through each unit of time (100 new individuals a year… 100, 200, 300, etc.). Or, populations may grow exponentially when resources are plentiful and competition is low (100, 200, 400, 800, etc.) Populations are kept in check by both density dependent and density independent factors. Density dependent forces become greater as a population grows, and can include competition and predation. This is self-regulation of the system. Independent forces, such as severe weather, act on populations regardless of density. *Carrying capacity* represents the population that an environment can sustain without suffering degradation. As a population grows beyond its carrying capacity, the environment is degraded. Eventually the population will decrease as survivorship goes down. Healthy ecosystems have higher carrying capacities as they offer more resources. As we degrade the environment, we reduce earth's capacity to support as many humans in future generations.

Keystone Species

Research reveals that some species play a disproportionate role on their environment even though they may exist in small numbers. Top-level predators (wolves, sharks, etc.) are often considered keystone species for this reason. They may control populations of many prey species through predation, thereby supporting a "balance" within the ecosystem. In 1966, researcher Robert Paine conducted a study where he removed *Pisaster*, a carnivorous sea star species,

from tide pools believing it would increase species diversity. Instead, he found that species diversity plummeted in their absence. *Pisaster* was found to be a keystone species that regulated the populations of other carnivorous gastropods. In the absence of *Pisaster*, the gastropods ate everything and drove many species locally extinct. Humans have long since waged a battle against many of our predators believing that fewer predators means more prey. We are now finding that is not necessarily the case. We catch a large quantity of top-level marine predators for food resulting in severely reduced populations with unclear impacts to marine ecosystems.

3. Energy Flows

Living systems are open systems that capture energy from the sun. The energy then flows through food webs as organisms eat each other. In the end, all the energy is released as thermal heat that dissipates into the environment, as heat is a byproduct of cellular metabolism. Primary producers (photosynthetic bacteria, algae, and plants) capture the sun's light energy through photosynthesis; a process where they construct molecules of glucose from water and carbon dioxide using the sun's light energy. Primary consumers (herbivores) then eat producers to gain energy. Then, secondary consumers (carnivores) eat the primary consumers for energy. Different types of decomposers (bacteria and fungi) gain their energy by "consuming" dead organisms and organic matter.

In this way, energy flows through ecosystems. However, the transfer of energy is not very efficient. Much of the energy is used at each trophic level to support metabolic processes, which ultimately result in the "loss" of energy in the form of heat. Only about 10% of the total energy from one trophic level transfers to the next level. Therefore a food chain can only support five or six trophic levels, most support even fewer, because at a certain point there is simply too little energy to support an additional level.

While food chains help us understand how energy flows through ecosystems, food webs are a better model representing the complexity of energy flow given that most organisms access their energy by eating more than one thing. Sustainable systems require only the amount of energy they can capture from the sun.

4. Cycles

Earth is a closed system where the total amount of matter is unchanging. The form matter takes changes as atoms are recombined into different compounds through chemical processes or as substances transform into different states. These cycles prevent the "dead-end" accumulation of important elements and molecules into forms unusable by living organisms. Three important cycles in nature define how substances, vital to life, cycle through ecosystems; they are the water cycle, the carbon cycle, and the nitrogen cycle.

The Water Cycle

The sun's energy ultimately drives the water cycle. Thermal heat from the sun (infrared light) evaporates water from liquid to vapor. Water vapor in the atmosphere circulates via predominate weather patters and eventually falls back to the ground as precipitation when vapor condenses upon cooling. The water then flows across land toward the ocean. Through this cycle, water moves through its different states and is made available to life across the planet.

The Carbon Cycle

Carbon represents one of the building blocks of life. It is an element present in all life forms on earth. Carbon is also stored in many abiotic forms such as limestone, fossil fuels, in the atmosphere as carbon dioxide (CO_2), and dissolved inorganic carbon in the oceans. Carbon cycles through the earth's systems as a result of chemical and biological processes that transform the carbon from one form to another. Producers, organisms at the bottom of the food chain, convert CO_2 into glucose through photosynthesis, all life forms metabolize sugar into CO_2 and water, we combust fossil fuels and other organic matter (wood) that releases CO_2 into the atmosphere, CO_2 is released from geologic processes like volcanoes and chemical decomposition of limestone, and carbon moves into and out of solution from the oceans. Through time the carbon balance can shift from stored forms to CO_2 in the atmosphere, thereby impacting climate systems.

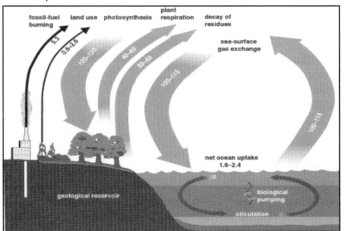

The Carbon Cycle. Carbon cycles from its stored form to CO_2 in the atmosphere. Currently, a larger than average amount of carbon is being released into the atmosphere due to human activities such as burning fossil fuels.

The Nitrogen Cycle

The element Nitrogen cycles through living and non-living systems and is crucial in certain macromolecules that represent the building blocks of cells. DNA and proteins, both require nitrogen, as does the pigment chlorophyll that plants use to capture light energy during photosynthesis. Most of the earth's nitrogen exists in its inorganic form as N_2 in the atmosphere (78% of our air is N_2). In this form, it is unusable by plants, though certain types of bacteria are capable of converting N_2 into forms usable by plants known as fertilizers (nitrification). *Rhizobium* is a genus of bacteria that live in the root nodules of legumes. They convert N_2 from the air into usable forms for the plant and the plant provides food in the form of

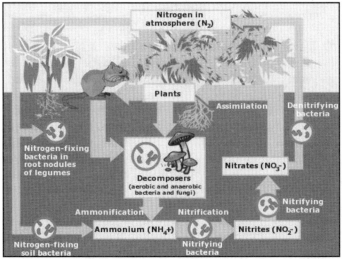

The Nitrogen Cycle. Nitrogen, an essential element for life, exists in abundance in the atmosphere and can be fixed for use by living organisms.

sugars to the bacteria in a mutualistic symbiotic relationship. Decomposers, mainly bacteria and fungi, convert organic waste from dead plants and animals or excrement back into forms usable by plants (ammonification). Other forms of bacteria denitrify nitrogen by converting forms usable by plants as fertilizer back into N_2 in the atmosphere. Certain agricultural and industrial processes release N_2O into the atmosphere, which results in acid rain. The accumulation of nitrogenous waste (animal waste from pig farms for instance) into ecosystems can create imbalances that result in large algae blooms and then die-offs that alter plant and animal communities.

5. Change (Also called Development)

All ecosystems develop and change through time. Physical factors like climate shift through time. Changes—along with many other types of selective pressures—drive evolutionary processes of change, as only organisms that possess adaptations for new environments can compete for limited resources. Communities themselves shift through biological succession as one community of organisms is replaced by another that better competes for resources under different environmental conditions. We must emphasize that change is inevitable. These changes can occur through highly variable scales of time. As individual humans with short life spans relative to geologic time, we struggle conceptualizing many of the changes earth's systems undergo.

Evolution

Individual organisms themselves do not evolve. Populations, however, evolve as the proportion of individuals within a population that possess a favorable and heritable trait increases through successive generations. In a process known as *natural selection*, selective pressures like competition, sexual selection, changing environments, predation, and disease select only the most fit individuals to survive. *Fitness* refers to those individuals best adapted to both survive and reproduce. Four principals define how natural selection drives evolution:

- There is genetic variation among individuals within all populations.
- Some of this variation is heritable and can be passed to successive generations.
- There are limited resources for any particular population and competition prevents all individuals from surviving and reproducing.
- Those individuals best adapted to their environment will live longer and reproduce more, thereby passing on their genes and traits to successive generations.

On a small scale this could mean that as a few generations pass, the percentage of individuals possessing a particular allele (distinct version of a gene) increases or decreases. This is considered a shift in allelic frequency. For example, when an antibiotic is applied to a culture of bacteria most will die, but a few with a variety of a gene (allele) that allows for resistance to the antibiotic will survive. These resistant strains then multiply and the total proportion of individuals with that allele has increased. That, by definition, is biological evolution.

On a large scale, a population may reveal more significant *phenotypic* changes. A phenotypic change is a change in an observable physical characteristic like a noticeable increase in bill size of finches with a changing food source. It is harder to conceptualize larger changes because it may take a very long time over many generations, but the process is the same.

Since changing environments act as pressures that drive the evolutionary process, we must consider whether living communities can "adapt" to changes humans impose. Biological evolution is a

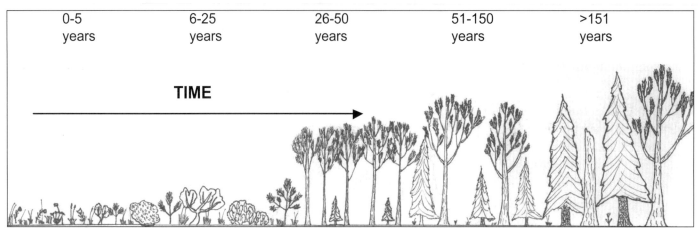

| 0-5 years | 6-25 years | 26-50 years | 51-150 years | >151 years |

TIME

Biological succession in a forest. After a catastrophic event like a forest fire kills nearly every organism in a landscape it takes many years for the forest to recover to its mature state. Initially, pioneer species begin to take back the charred earth. Then, more than one hundred years later, after a multitude of different species have taken root, the forest will eventually return to maturity.

slow process, especially for organisms with long generation times like ourselves. Changes brought on by humans including climate change, habitat alteration and destruction, the introduction of non-native species, and changes in natural fire regimes all impact organisms' ability to compete and reproduce. Some individuals simply lack the best traits for survival. When a species as a whole lacks well-adapted traits to a newly changed environment, they go extinct. Fossil records indicate that 99.9% of all species that have existed through time have gone extinct. Understanding how species adapt to changing environments helps us prioritize human behaviors that support biodiversity.

Change in Communities Through Time

Different species of plants and animals assemble into common communities. These communities are not stagnant through time. Biological succession describes the process of change that communities undergo as local conditions shift. This process happens over shorter time scales than biological evolution. Forest succession may begin after a fire kills all the vegetation and may occur over a period decades to a few hundred years. Initially, pioneer species, well adapted to open environments, colonize the open area. Then shrubs and eventually trees begin to sprout. The earliest tree species are those well adapted to high light. Later, in the understory of the first tree colonizers, shade tolerant trees will sprout. In this way, the assemblages of plants and animals shift through time. The assemblage of particular species creates the environment in which new and different species can colonize, resulting in a community change. The shift can be reset anytime a disturbance restarts the cycle. Human development and management of ecosystems has shifted the balance towards certain stages of succession at times. For example, we often increase the proportion of early succession forests by harvesting trees when they are younger, thereby decreasing the total proportion of older succession forests (old-growth).

We have also altered the interval at which natural fires influence forest ecosystems and consequently impacted the succession process. These changes impact the types and proportions of plant communities that are on earth such that ecosystems of today are very different than what may have existed only 100-200 years ago.

The Issue of Climate Change

Politics and societal pressures have confused the issue of climate change. Scientific data clearly supports earth's climate as continually changing. Earth has experienced extremes of heat and cold over billions of years. These changes usually occur slowly during periods of thousands of years. Climate fluctuates for numerous reasons that include external factors like solar intensity and changes in planetary orbits, and numerous internal factors that include oceanic and atmospheric systems, living systems, and geological processes like plate tectonics and volcanism.

Little question exists that humans have altered systems in ways that impact climate. The question remains to what degree are changes a result of human activities and how extensive the changes will be. The bottom line is that changing climate will have significant positive and negative impacts on humans. Humans, and all life forms, will have to adjust to new environmental factors as climate changes. Some of those adjustments may be costly and challenging.

The most significant human impact to climate systems is the transformation of carbon stored in fossil fuels to carbon in the atmosphere as carbon dioxide. CO_2 in the atmosphere retains thermal heat radiating from the earth's surface after being warmed by the sun. This essentially traps heat in our atmosphere similar to a greenhouse trapping heat within its walls. This is largely beneficial, since it prevents all of earth's heat energy from dissipating into space leaving earth to cold to support life. However, large increases in CO_2 over short time periods of time (284 ppm CO_2 in 1832 vs. 384 ppm CO_2 in 2007) may result in climate change occurring more quickly than it ever has before. That makes it difficult to predict how living systems and ecological processes will respond, and what the consequences to humans will be.

6. Dynamic Balance

Ecosystems are constantly changing, and there is no final equilibrium point. Given the interconnectedness within ecosystems, changes in one part of an ecosystem result in feedback from other parts. In this way, ecosystems bring themselves back into balance. Fluctuations, however, occur with certain tolerances. Very large or rapid changes may cause instability in ecosystem processes that result in system collapse.

These collapses result in new patterns of organization with new balances. Some changes result in negative feedback loops that ultimately slow the change down. Other changes result in positive feedback loops that exacerbate the change. For example, the melting of polar ice caps allows for greater absorption of solar radiation thereby heating ocean temperatures more and further speeding the melting of the ice caps. System collapses have occurred before in earth's history where significant environmental change or disturbance resulted in mass extinctions. Yet, as new patterns of organization form, new groups of organisms appear in the fossil record as a result of newly opened niches.

Human induced changes have the potential to disrupt ecological systems in a way that could result in collapse. Our challenge is to learn to apply basic principles of ecology in our ways of living to avoid abrupt changes that alter systems to quickly or extensively.

References

- Environmental Literacy Council
- Ecological Society of America
- Capra, Fritjof. 2005. *Speaking Nature's Language: Principles for Sustainability.* in Ecological Literacy: Educating Our Children for a Sustainable World. Edited by: Stone, M. K., & Zenobia B. Sierra Club Books, San Francisco. pp. 18-29.
- Hooper, D. U., F. S. Chapin, III, J. J. Ewel, A. Hector, P. Inchausti, S. Lavorel, J. H. Lawton, D. M. Lodge, M. Loreau, S. Naeem, B. Schmid, H. Setälä, A. J. Symstad, J. Vandermeer, and D. A. Wardle. 2005. Effects of biodiversity on ecosystem processes: implications for ecosystem management [ESA Public Affairs Office, Position Paper]. Ecological Society of America. Jamestown, ND: Northern Prairie Wildlife Research Center Online. http://www.npwrc.usgs.gov/resource/habitat/econsens/index.htm (Version 24AUG2006).
- S. Naeem, F.S. Chapin III, R. Costanza, Paul R. Ehrlich, Frank B. Golley, David U. Hooper,
- J.H. Lawton, Robert V. OíNeill, Harold A. Mooney, Osvaldo E. Sala, Amy J. Symstad, and David Tilman, 1999. Biodiversity and Ecosystem Functioning: Maintaining Natural Life Support Processes, *Issues in Ecology*, Ecological Society of America, Issue 4, fall.

CHAPTER THREE
SCIENCE CLASSES AND ACTIVITIES

ECOLOGICAL CONCEPTS PART I – SCALE, INTERCONNECTEDNESS, & ENERGY FLOW

See First: The Six Ecological Concepts

Learning Objectives - The Learner Will be Able to:
- Discuss why scale is important to understanding how events at one level impact systems at other levels.
- Identify different examples of how organisms interact in the course area.
- Discuss the importance of biodiversity in helping sustain resilient ecosystems.
- Describe how energy flows through an ecosystem and describe the impacts of disrupting a food web.
- Apply the concept of energy pyramids to decisions regarding food production and land resource use.

What is Ecology
The scientific study of the interactions that determine the distribution and abundance of organisms.

Scale
Living systems operate within other living systems (i.e. networks within networks). The same patterns of organization and interaction exist at all levels, yet the complexity may differ. Individuals interact with other individuals to form a population. Different populations interact with each other, but also within their ecosystem. What happens at one system level impacts other levels. Cancer may start from a mutation in one cell, but as it replicates out of control it affects tissues, then organs, and then the entire organism. A question in ecology may have significantly different answers when studied at different scales. Humans may be under-populated at the population scale in one place but are over-populated at the biosphere scale. Processes and change also occur on differing time scales. Bacteria adapt quickly to new selective pressures since they replicate quickly. Conversely, in some ecosystems soil requires hundreds of years to recover from a disturbance. If we understand the patterns of organization of one system, we can apply that knowledge to another level of scale.

Interconnectedness (Networks)
All organisms in an ecosystem are interconnected and derive their food and resources through relationships with other living organisms and the abiotic world (i.e., the web of life). All things are connected. Changes in one species or environment have impacts throughout the system.

Help students brainstorm the ways in which organisms interact. Generate examples of these relationships from your course area.

Competition – The struggles to access limited resources (light, food, water, minerals, mates, etc.) between individuals of the same species or between different species accessing the same resources.

Predation – When an individual of one species (predator) eats an individual of another species (prey). Grazing is predation of plants.

Symbiosis – Defines any close long-term relationship between two species. These relationships can be mutually beneficial (mutualism), beneficial to one species while the other is unaffected (commensalism), or beneficial to one species at the expense of the other (parasitism).

Brainstorm how organisms interact with their abiotic environment, e.g., accessing nutrients, impacts from climate, disturbances (fire and wind), accessing light, toxins, atmospheric changes, etc.

Populations impact each other. Given the interconnectedness of organisms between each other and the non-living world, populations within the web of life constantly change as their ability to access resources changes. As one population decreases, others may increase as they interact. Many populations of plants and animals have decreased as a result of human actions, while our own population increases.

It is important to discuss issues surrounding the loss of many top-level predators and the concept of a keystone species. Some species may have a more significant role in a community than others. Many top-level predators play a disproportionately important role in ecosystems. What we've learned by re-introducing wolves in Yellowstone is a great example as plants have recovered from less grazing pressure and pray populations are healthier. Ocean ecosystems are another prime example given that many of our prized fish are predators (tuna, swordfish, and sharks).

Biodiversity is a measure of variability at all levels of scale in an ecosystem; some examples are genetic, species, community, ecosystem, etc. A more complex network of species with overlapping functions is more resilient to environmental change, while a less complex network like a field planted with a mono-crop is less resilient and more susceptible to disease. While we often "manage" ecosystems for uniformity, we benefit from the stability and resiliency diversity affords us.

Challenge students to consider the impact of removing a species from the network? Brainstorm as many impacts as you can.

Energy Flow
Living systems are open systems through which energy flows. Life requires energy, and the sun is earth's primary energy source; 99% of energy for living organisms comes from the sun. A limited number get their energy from the earth's heat—think deep sea thermal vents and bacteria that live off sulfur compounds released by the vents.

A marine and terrestrial food chain. Energy flows up the chain of consumers to higher and higher trophic levels. Only about 10% of the energy stored in an organism is passed on to the next trophic level when it is consumed.

Describe a simple food chain and how energy transfers from one trophic level to the next (draw this for a visual). Energy flows in one direction and not all of an organism's energy transfers when it's eaten. Much energy is used during metabolism and "lost" as heat or cannot be eaten or digested. On average, only 10% of the energy from one trophic level is obtained from the next "higher" trophic level (the 10% rule).

A food web depicts the complexity of relationships between numerous species. Ask students what happens when one species is removed and discuss possibilities.

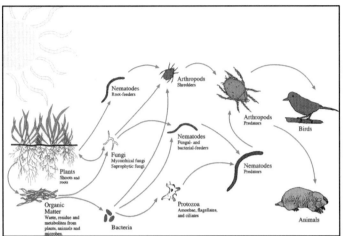

An example of a food web. A food web represents an ecosystem's interconnectedness more accurately than a food chain because it depicts the various relationships between organisms.

Applying an Ecological Pyramid to How We Eat

Use an ecological pyramid to demonstrate how 10% of the energy transfers from one trophic level to the next. You can also use biomass instead of energy (i.e., a human could build 1 Kg of new biomass by consuming 10 Kg of biomass from a lower trophic level (meat or plant)). These pyramids can also be applied in understanding how much life an ecosystem will support. If an ecosystem supports only a small base of autotrophs as a result of lack of water or nutrient rich soil, then what would you expect about the levels above it in the pyramid? How big will they be? How many levels will they have?

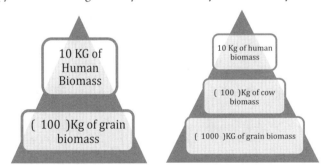

The food pyramid on the left represents a vegetarian diet and the one on the right a carnivorous diet. Due to trophic levels, it takes ten times more grain (and therefore land) to feed the carnivore.

Look at the following pyramids and think about the resources, such as the amount of land, required to grow the grain to support the growth of 10 Kg of human biomass (assume that it requires 1 acre of land to produce 100Kg of grain). Many scientists believe that the Earth cannot support a growing human population that survives on a meat-based diet without significant environmental consequences. Be careful here to not say eating meat is wrong, but simply point out that understanding this ecological concept may help us make more sustainable choices in the future. Also add that this example is overly simplistic, yet does a good job of explaining the concept. Eating lower on the food chain, in this example, allows us to use 10 times less land resources to gain the same nutrients.

Have students discuss arguments for or against the statement "Humans must eat lower on the food chain or there will be no room for people and wild ecosystems." Remember, that from a sustainability point of view, there is a difference between food resources derived from natural ecosystems versus those from controlled ecosystems, i.e., industrial agriculture and factory farming. The premise of an ecological pyramid is founded on the concept of energy flow through food chains. The fewer levels in the chain, the more efficient it is.

Conclusion

Have students draw three quick pictures that depict scale, interconnectedness, and energy flow. Give them 3-5 minutes. Extra points for an image that captures all three together! Have students briefly share what they come up with.

Transfer of Learning

- We can apply what we know from simpler scales of living systems to ecosystems for understanding how to live sustainably given that patterns of organization are the same.
- What species we choose to eat, protect, manage, etc., is important. Keystone species may have a disproportionately important impact on ecosystem structure, i.e., if these species disappear then ecosystems begin to unravel more significantly.
- How we choose to grow our food and harvest food impacts the web of life and the amount of resources we consume.

Assessment and Next Steps

- The Ecology Quiz Game is composed of questions that review much of this lesson and serves as a fun assessment for this class. It also covers other ecological functions not covered here, but that many students have seen in other academic settings.
- Revisit these concepts during other ES activities like ecological footprint, environmental ethics, and ecosystem services.
- Some classes to teach from here include ecological concepts part II, and specific, relevant, or pertinent topics (e.g., stream ecology).

References

- Environmental Literacy Council
- Ecological Society of America
- Capra, Fritjof. 2005. *Speaking Nature's Language: Principles for Sustainability.* in Ecological Literacy: Educating Our Children for a Sustainable World. Edited by: Stone, M. K., & Zenobia B. Sierra Club Books, San Francisco. pp. 18-29.
- S. Naeem, F.S. Chapin III, R. Costanza, Paul R. Ehrlich, Frank B. Golley, David U. Hooper,
- J.H. Lawton, Robert V. OfNeill, Harold A. Mooney, Osvaldo E. Sala, Amy J. Symstad, and David Tilman, 1999. Biodiversity and Ecosystem Functioning: Maintaining Natural Life Support Processes, *Issues in Ecology*, Ecological Society of America, Issue 4, fall.

ECOLOGICAL CONCEPTS PART II – CYCLES, CHANGE, AND DYNAMIC BALANCE

See First: The Six Ecological Concepts

Instructor Note – These concepts can easily be addressed within the context of other classes, e.g., change within geology, change and dynamic balance within the geologic timeline activity, change and dynamic balance within a glaciology class, cycles within nuggets on plants that are nitrogen fixers, or during a weather class that addresses the water cycle.

Learning Objectives - The Learner Will be Able to:

- Discuss ways in which ecosystems are dynamic and how humans impact ecosystem change, or how ecosystem change may impact humans.
- Explain the role natural selection plays in our ability to predict changes resulting from human impacts on ecosystems.
- Explain the role "cycles" play in ecosystems and how we can apply this knowledge to improve human sustainability on earth.
- Discuss the impact of rapid and large changes on earths living systems.

Change

Ecosystems are dynamic, but as humans we often view the world as static since we don't live long enough to see much change. It's important to help students understand the significant changes that earth undergoes with or without humans and how processes like natural selection determine which species are winners or losers in newly formed environments.

How does the earth and its living systems change? Climate changes as do landforms. Ecosystems also change through succession as one group of species replace another group, as demonstrated by the shift from a barren field to an old-growth forest. Species also evolve as those individuals in a population best adapted to the environment thrive while others dwindle. Changing physical factors like climate drive this process. Species also co-evolve, with changes in one species impacting changes in another. As species evolve, so do ecosystems; groupings of species that thrive change to fit new environmental conditions. Each of these changes may occur on different scales of time, but they all interact together.

Natural selection is a process where individuals in any population—who are all a bit different—with the best traits for survival and reproduction, live the longest, reproduce the most and pass on their genes. Through time certain traits are "selected" for by nature while others are lost since they provide no benefit and likely are just an added expense in terms of energy. Novel traits that arise may be selected for if they provide advantage resulting in evolutionary change.

Why is biodiversity important? Ecosystems high in species diversity and genetic diversity are more resilient to change. One pest can wipe out a monoculture of corn, but a field with numerous varieties of corn would likely have some surviving plants.

How can we help protect biodiversity? Guide students through a brainstorm of ways we can sustain and promote biodiversity.

On the other hand, catastrophic changes, such as mass extinctions, have created open niches that provide opportunity for novel traits to take hold and new species to evolve that occupy those niches. Mammal diversity exploded after the Cretaceous extinction event when dinosaurs disappeared. On a geologic time scale, change is neither good nor bad. A mass extinction would significantly impact humans, however, so catastrophic change is bad for us!

Humans are changing our environments at what may be an unprecedented rate. What organisms will have traits suitable for new environments? What organisms will be able to either adapt to new environments or migrate to suitable environments? How will changes in our biosphere like biodiversity loss impact humans? Physical evidence supports the occurrence of 5 mass extinctions in earth's history. Most scientists say we're currently in the 6th mass extinction with extinction rates 100 to 1000 times higher than what would be the "normal background rate."

Cycles

Earth is a closed system in terms of matter; no new matter enters, it just cycles. Matter including important nutrients, elements, and molecules crucial to living systems cycles through the web of life. If they did not cycle they would accumulate in forms unusable by living systems. Ultimately, either directly or indirectly the sun's energy drives these cycles by supporting life forms.

How does water cycle through ecosystems? The sun's energy evaporates water to vapor that then circulates in the atmosphere before precipitating back to the ground as rain or snow. In this way freshwater is made available to different living systems. Draw a diagram of the water cycle.

How does carbon cycle through ecosystems? Carbon is the backbone element of organic molecules crucial to life. It exists in many forms. Most of it is stored in rock such as limestone or dissolved in the ocean. It's also stored in the molecules of living organisms, fossil fuels, and as carbon dioxide (CO_2) in the air. Biological processes like photosynthesis (converts CO_2 into organic molecules) and respiration (converts the carbon in sugars back to CO_2), physical processes like volcanoes, and human actions like the burning of fossil fuels all transform carbon from one form to another. The amount of carbon in the atmosphere as CO_2 impacts climate systems by trapping in heat radiated by the earth. This means that what we do as humans impacts climate and consequently all living systems. Draw a diagram of the carbon cycle (p. 14).

How does nitrogen cycle through ecosystems?[1] Nitrogen is a necessary element in macromolecules vital to living organisms like nucleic acids (DNA, RNA), amino acids (building blocks for proteins), and chlorophyll (pigment used by plants for photosynthesis). Nitrogen cycles from inorganic forms (N_2 in the air) to forms usable by plants as fertilizer, which can then be eaten by other organisms and move through food webs. Bacteria convert nitrogen from the air into nitrates usable by plants through a series of biological processes. Other bacteria convert nitrates back to N_2. Some bacteria and fungi convert organic matter (poop, dead tissue, etc.) into nitrates as well. In this way, nitrogen is cycled making it available to living systems. Human created pollutants sometimes contribute high levels of nitrogen into ecosystems disrupting the web of life by supporting large algae blooms that take advantage of nitrogen boosts. Draw a diagram of the nitrogen cycle (p. 14).

Dynamic Balance

Ecosystems are constantly changing. There is no final equilibrium point. Yet, given the interconnectedness within ecosystems, changes in one part of an ecosystem result in feedback from other parts, and in this way bring themselves back into balance. Negative feedback loops slow down change, while positive feedback loops exacerbate change. For example, melting ice results in increased absorption of the sun's energy, which warms more water and melts more ice.

1 See "Creating Conscientious Nature Nuggets class" for a "Nature Nugget" on the Nitrogen cycle.

Fluctuations occur within tolerance limits, and large or rapid changes can result in temporary collapse that leads to new patterns of organization with new balances.

While system collapses have occurred before on earth (mass extinctions), they stand to be problematic for humans. Human induced changes have the potential to disrupt ecological systems, which could result in collapse.

Conclusion (Conclude with some open-ended review questions)

- How does the earth change and what does that mean for humans?
- Is there a relationship between natural selection and biodiversity? Why are these concepts important?
- What are three cycles that are important to life?
- How can we use knowledge of cycles to improve our sustainability? Think about farming, preventing water pollution, and slowing the transformation of carbon to CO_2.
- Are ecosystems truly balanced? What does that mean to us? How do fluctuations in various parts of the ecosystem affect other populations or ecosystems?

Transfer of Learning

- Composting is a controlled way to convert organic waste into usable fertilizers for farming that capitalizes on the nitrogen cycle.
- Any plant you see in the field in the pea family shares a mutualistic symbiosis with bacteria that can take nitrogen in the air and convert it to forms usable by the plants. We can apply this in our own garden to enrich the soil with nitrogen.
- Choosing lifestyles and developing technologies that reduce our CO_2 inputs into the atmosphere will slow our impact on climate systems.
- Every decision we make in some ways interacts with the living systems around us.
- Change induced by humans may not be "wrong", but it will impact future generations along with other living systems. We must decide what to do about that reality.

Assessment and Next Steps

- The Ecology Quiz Game is composed of questions that review much of this lesson and serves as a fun assessment tool for this class. It also covers other ecological functions not covered here, but that many students have seen in other academic settings.
- Revisit these concepts during other ES activities like calculating your ecological footprint, environmental ethics, and ecosystem services.

References

- Environmental Literacy Council
- Ecological Society of America
- "Human Population Growth and Extinction". Center for Biological Diversity.
- S. Naeem, F.S. Chapin III, R. Costanza, Paul R. Ehrlich, Frank B. Golley, David U. Hooper,
- J.H. Lawton, Robert V. OíNeill, Harold A. Mooney, Osvaldo E. Sala, Amy J. Symstad, and David Tilman, 1999. Biodiversity and Ecosystem Functioning: Maintaining Natural Life Support Processes, *Issues in Ecology*, Ecological Society of America, Issue 4, fall.
- Capra, Fritjof. 2005. *Speaking Nature's Language: Principles for Sustainability.* in Ecological Literacy: Educating Our Children for a Sustainable World. Edited by: Stone, M. K., & Zenobia B. Sierra Club Books, San Francisco. pp. 18-29.

HOW TO POOP IN THE WOODS
By John Gookin PhD

The ultimate goal of this class is to impart enough knowledge to students so they can poop in the woods properly while applying the LNT principles. Connecting these principles to ecosystem functioning helps provide valid reasons for good poop etiquette and is an opportunity for transferring these principles to other types of waste disposal back home. As with many new skills, this one must be revisited, especially as you enter new environments during your course that naturally have different waste disposal concerns. Instructors should know every detail of the accompanying full-page soil diagram (inside front cover), in order to be able to use basic ecological concepts to explain why we alter our cathole practices in different environments.

Learning Objectives - The Learner Will be Able to:

- Dispose of waste properly and give at least one reason for each general rule, e.g., 200 ft from water to prevent surface flow from resulting in contamination (remember the that our practices reflect both ecological and social impacts).
- Describe soil as an ecosystem with both living and non-living components that provide habitat and play an important role in nutrient cycling.
- Relate that proper disposal of human waste best allows ecosystem processes to breakdown and transform harmful pathogens into healthy soil. Connect this process to the concept of sustainability.
- Apply human waste disposal principles in a variety of ecosystem types.
- Transfer principles of waste disposal to other types of waste they create at home.

Motivation

Our poop has over 100 known types of germs in it that can get other people sick and harm the environment. Proper disposal of our poop allows natural composting systems to get rid of the "bad" germs and actually uses our poop to enrich the soil. It takes good poop disposal techniques to make this difference.

Soil

Soil is a combination of 1) mineral matter of different sizes (sand, silt, and clay) decomposed from parent material rock through physical and chemical weathering processes, 2) decomposed plant and animal matter, and 3) living organisms including bacteria, fungi, plants, and myriad other invertebrates and vertebrates. The combination of the living and non-living components of soil, and their relationships, form a soil ecosystem. Ecological processes in the soil allow for breakdown and transformation of organic molecules, like human waste, and dead plant and animal matter, into forms usable by plants as fertilizer. During this process, harmful pathogenic bacteria in human waste are outcompeted by soil bacteria, making soil a "natural filter" for pathogens that might otherwise spread disease.

Demonstration

Show students how to find natural toilet paper, choose a cat hole location, dig a cat hole, mix your stuff up, and disguise your hole. Many of these points can be covered during the demonstration.

Location: Surface contamination occurs when rainwater washes contaminants from the ground's surface into the water supply. Poop 200 feet (60 meters) away from running water to avoid surface contamination of water sources. Poop on flat soil, not on a slope, so

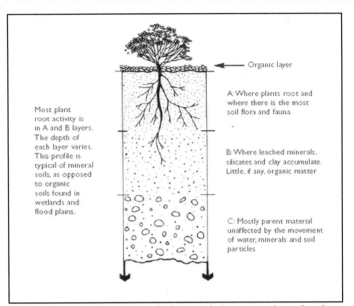

Most plant root activity is in A and B layers. The depth of each layer varies. This profile is typical of mineral soils, as opposed to organic soils found in wetlands and flood plains.

Organic layer

A: Where plants root and where there is the most soil flora and fauna

B: Where leached minerals, silicates and clay accumulate. Little, if any, organic matter

C: Mostly parent material unaffected by the movement of water, minerals and soil particles

Soil Layers. In rich organic soil, dig a cathole six to eight inches down where the poop will encounter the most decomposers. Try mixing the poop with loose soil to accelerate its decomposition.

rainwater won't wash your deposit away. Stay at least 200 feet (60 meters) from camps and trails to avoid local concentrations of human waste.

Soil: Moist dark soil is ideal for composting feces. Well-drained soil tends to be moist but not soaking wet. In general, darker soils are the soils with more biological activity. Arid soils can compost feces, but the biologically active layer is in the top of the mineral soil. Local techniques include utilizing the more highly developed soils in the shade of trees or any micro-ecosystem that seems to support more obvious plant growth or darker soil. Roots in your cathole are a good sign of biological activity because of the biologically active rhizosphere—an area of soil near roots that is influenced by their secretions. In sandy areas, look for a rhizosphere near the edges of cover plants.

Depth: Soil has layers. The best biologic agents that break down poop are found in the topsoil layer, which is below the rotting sticks and leaves lying on the ground (the humus layer) and above the light colored ground up rocks (the mineral soil). The topsoil layer actually includes a mix of humus and ground minerals. In many forests, this topsoil layer is about 6-8" below the surface.

Mixing: If you use a stick to mix some topsoil into your poop, the microorganisms break down your poop and get rid of the "bad" bacteria about ten times as quickly.

Fun Facts

Scientists who study fecal decomposition (poopologists?) mix human poop with different types of soils and with different amounts of moisture, and they put these recipes in hundreds of Dixie cups. Then they time how long it takes for different combinations to have the "good" bacteria out-compete the "bad" bacteria. These are the folks who tell us we want moist rich topsoil that is well mixed with our poop. The best recipe results in clean compost within 3 months. The worst recipe results in clean compost after 2 years. Poop "contains about nine times more living bacteria, bacterial cells, than the body contains human cells. So in a manner of speaking, we are 10% human and 90% poop." (Dubner, 2011)

Transfer of Learning

Municipal water treatment and composting work the same way as the break down of poop in the soil. We actually nurture the growth of particular types of bacteria in these processes to breakdown large amounts of organic waste.

While different places in the world will have varying soil types with varying capacities to decompose human waste, the principles remain the same. Look for soil that has an organic component away from trails, camps, and water (200 ft.) Some areas with high recreational use require that we simply carry out our waste with us.

References

- WEN
- LNT skills & ethics booklets- this series includes waste disposal practices for over a dozen environments
- Cilimburg, Amy; Monz, Chris; & Kehoe, Sharon. (2000). Wildland Recreation and Human Waste: A Review of Problems, Practices, and Concerns. *Environmental Management*, 25(6):587–598.
- Tilton, Buck, (2003) Leave No Trace Master Educator Notebook.
- Dubner, Stephen J, (2011, March, 4) General format. Retrieved from http://www.freakonomics.com/2011/03/04/freakonomics-radio-the-power-of-poop/

CHANGE – AN ECOLOGICAL CONCEPT

Change in ecosystems remains one of the hardest concepts for us to understand because, as individuals, we only see short snapshots in time. Yet we live in a changing world where those changes directly influence us. Furthermore, humans are imposing new and rapid changes on ecological systems and processes that will also impact us. Understanding the processes of change in ecological systems helps us better understand our role as humans and how we can make sustainable choices.

Learning Objectives - The Learner Will be Able to:

- Explain three ways that earth changes through time.
- Discuss major changes that have occurred in earth's history.
- Discuss the relevance human actions have on changing earth and its physical and biological processes through the concept of Dynamic Balance.

Earth's History (See chart on page 24)

Walk a geologic timeline with your students to explore major geologic and biologic events throughout earth's history. Use a 100-foot (30 meter) piece of rope or series of p-cord pieces tied together, or pace off a hundred feet (average pace is close to 1.5 feet (.5 meters) per step, so 65-70 steps). Don't worry about accuracy; The take home message is how much time has passed and how little of it contains what we are familiar with. Mark the beginning of the following time periods along your timeline.

- 100 ft. (30m) - Beginning of the Precambrian - Formation of Earth – 4600 MYA (4.6 billion years ago)
- 11.8 ft. (3.6m) - Beginning of the Paleozoic era
- 5.4 ft. (1.6m) - Beginning of the Mesozoic era
- 1.4 ft. (.43m) - Beginning of the Cenozoic era and beginning of the Tertiary period
- 0.04 ft. (1.2cm) - Beginning of the Quaternary period (1.8 million years long) within the Cenozoic era

As you walk along the timeline, starting with the past, you can highlight some of the most interesting changes that have occurred in earth's history using the information from the table Earth's History on the following page. Highlight the mass extinctions, evolution of major groups, and the general theme of change. Remember to highlight that major changes like mass extinctions open up new environments for other organisms to evolve. For example mammals were able to flourish only after the dinosaur extinction 65 million years ago.

"We are surrounded with people who think that what we have been doing for one fortieth of the [last] second can go on indefinitely. They are considered normal, but they are stark raving mad."
-David Brower

Planetary Change
Now that you've looked at earth's history, brainstorm a list of ways that earth has changed throughout time. By the end of the brainstorm you should have come up with at least: atmospheric composition, land masses as plates shift, plant and animal composition and distribution, climate, sea levels, and land forms.

Processes That Drive Change
Next have students brainstorm the processes that drive these changes, divided into three categories:
Biologic processes: Natural selection, biological succession, photosynthesis, cellular respiration
Physical processes: Plate tectonics, volcanoes emit CO_2 and other gases, formation and decomposition of some rock types shift the CO_2 balance in the atmosphere (most of earth's CO_2 is stored in limestone).
Human influences – Fossil fuel burning, pollution, habitat alteration, introduction of non-native species, waste production, poor farming practices.

Human Influenced Change
- A 6th mass extinction resulting in biodiversity loss.
- Climate change – mainly as a result of increases of green house gases in the atmosphere
- We can expect evolutionary changes in organisms as populations evolve to new environmental conditions, which may happen slowly for some (humans) and quickly for others (i.e., antibiotic resistant bacteria).

The Connection Between Dynamic Balance and Change
As we noted earlier, ecosystems are constantly changing; there is no final equilibrium point. Yet given the interconnectedness within ecosystems, changes in one part of an ecosystem result in feedback from other parts. In this way, ecosystems bring themselves back into balance. Fluctuations, however, can only occur with certain tolerances. Very large or rapid changes may cause instability in ecosystem processes that result in system collapse. These collapses result in new patterns of organization with new balances. The rapid changes humans have made to Earth's systems are resulting in the planets 6th mass extinction event (an example of a change that exceeded tolerance limits). When change is viewed through the lens of geologic time, it is neither good nor bad. However, rapid change resulting in a mass extinction will present humanity with many challenges that have significant consequences to us, both good and bad. Our challenge is to learn to apply basic principles of ecology in our ways of living to avoid abrupt changes that alter systems to quickly or extensively.

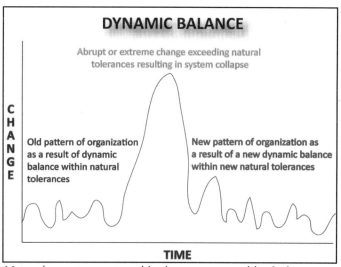

Major changes in ecosystems like the one represented by the large curve in this graph can result in ecosystem collapse. After collapse, the ecosystem will seek a new equilibrium or dynamic balance.

Conclusion
- Name three ways earth has changed throughout its history?
- What processes drive these changes?
- How are humans influencing these processes/changes?
- Drive home the message that earth is dynamic. The physical characteristics of earth change through time, as does life on earth. The two cannot be separated. Nor can humans be separated from the changes that earth undergoes. We must attempt to live sustainably and avoid exacerbating changes as these changes will prove challenging for us.

Transfer of Learning
- Change has always been a part of natural systems on earth.
- Humans are influencing types and extent of change.
- The changes we are influencing (climate, land cover, habitat alteration, distribution of non-native species) may be quite rapid and have long-term impacts to earth's systems and humanity.
- It may be less a question of right or wrong, and more a question of how will we handle this change?

Assessment and Next Steps
Have students identify, as part of their observation journals, changes that ecosystems you visit are undergoing. How will organisms and other ecosystem factors continue to change as a result?

Highlighting these changes is a great stepping-stone for addressing more specifically how and why particular changes occur. Students may ask questions about the greenhouse effect, the ozone layer, etc. The section of the EEN that covers ecological concepts will be helpful addressing these issues.

Use this table to construct your timeline. Emphasize the mass extinctions and major evolutionary events.

Eon	Era	Period	MYA	Feet on timeline	Events
Phanerozoic	Cenozoic - Age of Mammals	Quaternary	0-1.8	0.04 (0.5 inches)	Evolution of humans to modern *Homo sapiens sapiens* (900,000 YA), Neanderthals (130,000 YA), Last ice age (15,000 YA)
		Tertiary	1.8-65	1.4	First hominids (tribe that now includes two species of chimpanzee and humans) 7 MYA, First Australopithecus (possible human ancestor) 3.9 MYA, mammals diversify, climate begins cooling (23 MYA), Laramie Orogeny ends (55 MYA), Alps begin forming (55 MYA), first primates (40 MYA), first apes (25 MYA)
	Meso-zoic - Age of Reptiles	Cretaceous	65-144	3.1	Cretaceous-Tertiary Extinction - 75% of all species including all dinosaurs (66 MYA), first primates (65 MYA), first flowering plants (130 MYA)
		Jurassic	144-206	4.5	First birds (150 MYA), dinosaurs diversify, break up of Gondwana (144 MYA)
		Triassic	206-248	5.4	Triassic-Jurrassic Extinction (many marine organisms and large amphibians went extinct), first mammals (215 MYA), first dinosaurs (230 MYA), Pangaea divides into Gondwana and Laurasia (245 MYA)
	Paleozoic	Permian	248-290	6.3	Permian-Triassic Extinction - largest extinction event - 95% of life (251 MYA), reptiles diversify, land masses unite into Pangaea (253 MYA)
		Pennsylva-nian	290-323	7.0	First reptiles (320 MYA), large scale trees related to what are now club-mosses, plant matter from Pennsylvanian and Mississippian resulted in large coal deposits
		Mississip-pian	323-354	7.7	Seed ferns - large fern-like trees that had gymnosperm like seeds, major diversification of insects
		Devonian	354-417	9.1	Late Devonian Extinction - 70% of all species - lasted 20 MY, jawed-fishes (bony fish) diversify (410 MYA), first amphibians (375 MYA)
		Silurian	417-443	9.6	Ordivician-Silurian Extinction - 2nd largest loss of life, first vascular plants invade land, first sharks (438 MYA)
		Ordovician	443-490	10.7	First green plants and fungi on land
		Cambrian	490-543	11.8	Major diversification of animal phyla, first jawless fishes (first chordates)
Protero-zoic	Precambrian (this is a common name for the period of time prior to the Cambrian Period)		543-2500	54.3	Atmosphere becomes oxygenic (2050 MYA), first Protist complex single-celled organisms (1800 MYA), first multi-celled organisms (800 MYA)
Archean			2500-3800	82.6	First oxygen producing photosynthetic bacteria (3600 MYA), first simple celled organisms (probably bacteria or archeans (3800 MYA)
Hadean			3800-4600	100.0	Formation of the earth, no free oxygen present (4540 MYA)

David Brower compares geological time to the six days of creation in the Genesis story. On the 6th day about:

4 p.m. – Big reptiles appear.

9 p.m. – Redwoods appear; big reptiles are gone.

11:57 p.m. – Humankind appears.

11:59:45 p.m. – Jesus is born.

A fortieth of a second before midnight – The Industrial Revolution begins.

NATURAL SELECTION: A DRIVING FORCE OF CHANGE

See First: The Six Ecological Concepts

Learning Objectives - The Learner Will be Able to:

* Explain how natural selection results in populations adapting to changing environments.
* Identify adaptations in local organisms.
* Extrapolate how changes in an environment might impact particular organisms.

Class Outline

Have students, in groups of two, choose a plant or animal to observe (it is recommended to combine active field observation if possible with potential background reading). Once they identify their specimen have them brainstorm answers to the following questions:

* How many do you see or have you seen in the landscape around you?
* What environmental factors may limit this organism's survival and reproduction, i.e., what are its selective pressures?
* How does it reproduce? Does it have many offspring or few? Do many of the offspring die or do most survive? Speculate if you have to.
* What adaptations does the organism have?
* How does it handle winter/summer extremes?
* Is the individual you found "winning" or not in the fitness sense?
* Have each group share their findings.

Basic Terminology

Ecological niche – The environment (location, habitat, life history, etc.) in which an individual successfully competes for resources. Occasionally described as how an organism "makes a living." The *Competitive Exclusion Principle* states that no two species can occupy the same niche for an extended time. Multiple species of warblers may nest and access food in the same species of tree; they will choose different places within the tree, thereby differentiating their niches so they do not overlap.

Adaptations – Advantageous traits that are heritable from one generation to the next. They can be physical characteristics or physiological ones like resistance to a particular disease.

Fitness – The measure of an individual's ability to compete for limited resources in its niche and to reproduce. Fitness implies the ability to reproduce and pass on your adaptations.

Natural Selection – The process that selects individuals within a population best adapted to access resources and reproduce. Even within a population of the same species of organism, individuals vary. Bigger or smaller, stronger or weaker, better eyesight or worse, bigger bill or smaller, darker fur or lighter, more effective immune system or less effective. The combination of all traits determines how well any individual can survive and reproduce. Natural selection is just a way to explain why some traits get passed on—even intensified—while others disappear. Evolution is not random. Only advantageous traits are selected. The origin of the trait may have been from a random gene mutation that resulted in something different—a bigger beak—but the selection of that trait to remain is certainly not random. If it doesn't improve your fitness, you'd expect that trait to dwindle in a population through time. Natural selection may drive adaptive evolution or simply maintain the status quo, especially in environments that are changing very little.

Survivorship - A collection of strategies or adaptations species have for reproducing. Plants may produce thousands of seeds, while only a few survive (type I), while humans produce few offspring, but survival is high (type III) Each has its advantages and disadvantages in particular environments under particular circumstances.

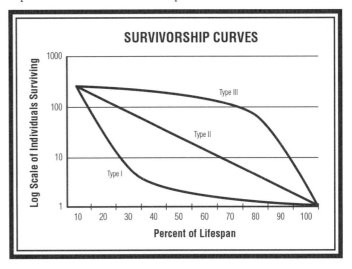

What role does natural selection play as earth changes through time? As environments change through time, individuals with traits that are advantageous become the new winners, even though they may have been poorly adapted in previous conditions. Through many generations, a shifting environment may drive a trait to "amplify." Warming climates with drier air continuously select individuals from populations with the best adaptations for those conditions. If fuzzy white hairs help with dry air, then as the air gets drier, individuals with more fuzzy white hairs may live longer and reproduce more.

Now, provide an example of a realistic environmental change. Tell students it will be 5 degrees warmer on average but with greater extremes: hotter-hots and colder-colds. Have students speculate the changes that might occur in this population of individuals in their groups for a few minutes?

* Will certain traits be selected for or amplified? Which ones?
* Will the population migrate somewhere? Plants may shift up or down in elevation or north or south in latitude. Animals may hibernate for longer or shorter time periods.
* Could this population be pushed to extinction?

Have groups share some of their thoughts and help them speculate. It doesn't matter if they are right or wrong. Just help them think.

Now is a great time to do the Timeline Walk Activity (see "Change" class). It demonstrates that the earth has changed dramatically throughout its history. The types of plants and animals that exist on earth have changed as a result. In the end, it is all about having the best traits in the conditions of a particular environment (climate, land forms, the other organisms around both of the same species or different species, atmospheric composition, etc.). A short reading, like Aldo Leopold's "Thinking Like a Mountain," in <u>A Sand County Almanac</u> makes for another thoughtful ending.

Conclusion

The earth is dynamic and ever changing. To that end, natural selection defines the process of how individuals with the best adaptations survive and reproduce to pass on their traits. Changing environments select new winners for survival.

Natural Selection will determine the winners and losers from new conditions created by the changes humans are causing. Humans will be directly impacted by all these changes, as we are part of the Web of Life.

Transfer of Learning

Ask students how understanding natural selection may help us understand what to do to mitigate some of the human induced changes to earth? (We may have to make difficult land management decisions to protect biodiversity to mitigate climate change impacts. This may mean moving species to new locations where they'll survive given they may not have fast enough migration times.)

Ask students whether we are still evolving? Watch out, this one can be contentious. The answer is yes. Certainly our culture (technology, access to resources, definitions of beauty, etc.) impacts how we evolve, but biological evolution cannot be avoided. There will always be change and individuals within populations—including humans—react differently to different pressures. Some people show resistance to HIV while others show none. We will expect those with a natural resistance to be the "winners" given the HIV epidemic.

Assessment and Next Steps

- Participation in the group activity is one way to assess this lesson.
- You might also give a journal prompt with 10 minutes of writing time at the end of class for students to address one of the transfer of learning questions.
- You can provide the details of a particular environment and have students design a "well-adapted" species. What are its physical traits? How does it access food? How does it protect itself? Have them draw and label a diagram.
- As the course progresses, ask students why questions. Why is that plant right there? What adaptations does that bug have and why? You need not have the answers; just help students wonder.
- If proctoring or changing ecosystems on your course, revisit this class on different sections.
- See "Ecology Quiz Game Questions" for additional questions to test for comprehension and transference.

References

- The Origin of Species by Charles Darwin - Chapter 4, Natural Selection
- Natural Selection- Modeling for Understanding in Science Education, University of Wisconsin
- Natural Selection from University of Berkeley education website

ECOLOGY QUIZ GAME QUESTIONS

These questions can be used for a quiz game assessment or general learning opportunity. Even if you have not taught all the content you can use this quiz, as most students will be familiar with terms. It is also a great opportunity for teachable moments to elaborate on points. The questions are organized into categories discussed within the NOLS ecological concepts curriculum and loosely have the feel of the TV game show *Jeopardy*. The questions may also serve as a guide for creating your own ecology class that emphasizes concepts most interesting to you or as a way to assess knowledge on other classes in this notebook.

What is Ecology?

- _____ is the study of interactions amongst organisms with their environment that determine their distribution and abundance – *What is ecology?*
- These are *non-living* factors that interact with organisms – *What are abiotic factors?*
- _____, _____, & _____ are three examples of abiotic factors - *What are soil, climate, air composition, nutrient availability, etc?*

Scale

- When looking at scales of ecology, the ecosystem scale is the first level to gain these factors that communities do not include – *What are abiotic factors?*
- Give an example of how one question in ecology might be answered differently if explored at different scales – *Human population at the community level could be low while at the biosphere level it is quite high.*
- Give an example of how ecological processes can occur at extremely different time scales – *Bacteria evolve over periods of minutes to hours, while human populations require hundreds of years. Biological succession occurs over hundreds of years, while geologic processes occur over thousands of years.*

Interconnectedness

- _____ is the habitat an organism occupies and the role it plays there. *What is an ecological niche?*
- Individuals of the same or different species _____ for limited resources - *What is compete?*
- This ecological interaction involves one organism living on or in another in order to obtain food and/or shelter, and negatively impacts its host (give example from course area for bonus) - *What is parasitism?*
- This ecological interaction involves one organism living on or in another in order to obtain food and/or shelter, and neither positively nor negatively impacts its host (give example from course area for bonus) - What is commensalism?
- This ecological interaction involves two organisms living in a close relationship where each benefits from the other (give example from course area for bonus) - *What is mutualism?*
- Mutualism, commensalism, and parasitism are all examples of close associations between organisms of different species also known as _____ - *What is symbiosis or symbiotic relationships?*
- Competition between individuals of the same species and gender where males or females compete for their mates is termed _____.- *What is sexual selection? Bonus points for a good example like the beautiful feathers on a male Peacock or the mating song of a male bird. It is also a driving evolutionary force described by Darwin like natural selection.*
- The population and health of these *species* help reveal the overall health and extent of an ecosystem type (try to give an example from your course area as a bonus) - *What is an indicator or keystone species? The Spotted Owl may be the most famous and political example.*
- Explain why biodiversity is important. *Biodiversity in all its forms (ecosystem, species, and genetic) makes biological systems more resilient to change. Each organism, ecosystem or gene, in all of their varieties, provide differences that may endow benefit for survival as our world continues to change.*
- Density dependent factors such as _____ increase as a population grows - *What is competition, disease or predation?*
- _____ is an example of a density independent factor for populations - *What is weather or climate?*
- A population equilibrium where births equal deaths or the maximum population a species in a certain environment can sustain - *What is carrying capacity?*
- True or false with an explanation: Carrying capacity for a species does not change through time. *False, it changes as other factors change. As we alter habitat, we reduce Earth's carrying capacity for certain species and increase it for others.*

- These species compete very aggressively and sometimes colonize unused niches (bonus points for examples) - *What are exotic or invasive species?*
- Humans are currently growing at this type of growth rate - *What is exponential growth?*

Energy Flow
- All living organisms need it - *What is energy?*
- A Weta (NZ bird) eating an arthropod that grazes on leaves that fell from trees that photosynthesize represents a _____ - *What is a food chain?*
- While a food chain shows how energy moves from one organism to another, a _____ is really a better representation to show the interrelated complexity between organisms in an ecosystem – *What is food web?*
- Energy always moves from _____ to _____ along a food chain. *What is from producers to consumers?*
- Explain why the removal of one species from a food web might be significant - *That species is food for other species. It may also play some role in an important cycle that no other organism plays like decomposition.*
- These organisms obtain their food by eating other animals - *What are carnivores?*
- These organisms obtain their energy by eating plants - *What are herbivores?*
- (2 parts) This process allows plants to build sugar molecules using the suns energy, water, and carbon dioxide. And, these organisms are called _____ - *What is photosynthesis and what are primary producers?*
- _____ is an example of a (use your location) primary consumer - *What is a ...? (deer, grazers)*
- _____ is an example of a (use your location) secondary consumer - *What is a ...? (carnivores)*
- These organisms play a crucial role in recycling plant and animal tissue into minerals that plants can use (name and example) - *What are decomposers like bacteria?*
- Each one of these represents a step along a food chain where energy is transferred - *What is a trophic level?*
- Given that no energy transfer is 100% efficient, this percentage represents the average efficiency of energy transfer from one trophic level to the next - *What is 10%*
- Based on the 10% rule, explain why a strictly meat based diet requires more land resources than a strictly vegetarian diet ecologically speaking. *In theory, eating strictly meat would use 10 times the land resources over eating strictly vegetarian since there is an additional level in this food chain that decreases the total energy transfer ten fold requiring tens time the land to get the same energy.*
- Certain species, termed _____, play a disproportionate role in a food web - *What is a keystone species? Many top-level predators play important role in ecosystems (wolves, sharks, etc.)*

Change
- This is the one constant about ecosystems on Earth – *What is they are always changing or are dynamic?*
- This process refers to changes in living community structure and function through time – *What is biological succession?*
- This type of succession occurs on a new substrate like volcanic rock – *What is primary succession?*
- (2 part) This type of succession occurs in previously vegetated soils following periodic disturbances such as _____ - *What is secondary succession and forest fires/wind/insect infestation?*

- Certain species, termed _____, specialize in colonizing areas soon after disturbances occur - *What are pioneer species?*
- Climate change (global warming in this case) is likely to have this generic impact on distribution of species through time – *What is moving towards the poles and to higher elevations? Bonus points for an explanation of why.*
- The ability to leave many offspring relative to others – *What is fitness?*
- A Darwinian process that explains how species evolve environmental adaptations – *What is Natural Selection?*
- Why understanding natural selection may be important to issues like climate change – *What is can organisms adapt to changing climate fast enough?*
- Four Important Points of Natural Selection are:
  – *All populations have variations (bigger hands vs. smaller).*
  – *Some variations are heritable and can be passed from generation to the next.*
  – *These variations provide some individuals with greater fitness (ability to share genes) in a world with limited resources.*
  – *Those that are most fit share their genes with future generations allowing populations to evolve adaptations through time.*

Cycles
- In the Nitrogen Cycle, _____ alter large organic molecules in dead plant and animal tissues into usable forms of nitrogen for plants called _____ - *What are bacteria and nitrates?*
- These two biological factors play an important role in the carbon cycle - *What are photosynthesis and respiration?*
- This human action is currently altering the carbon balance on Earth - *What are burning fossil fuels?*
- This process traps in heat radiated from the earth's surface after having been warmed from the sun, thereby preventing the earth from freezing, yet also resulting in recent global temperature increases - *What is the greenhouse effect?*
- (2 part) The _____ provides energy to drive this hydrologic cycle - *What are the sun and the water cycle?*

Dynamic Balance
- Five of these massive changes have occurred in geologic history when significant change to earth's systems have exceeded tolerances for bringing themselves back into balance – *What are mass extinctions?*
- _____ are a group of organisms that gained an opportunity to diversify when dinosaurs went extinct 65 million years ago – *What are mammals?*
- _____ is a type of system feedback that results in even more change – *What is a positive feedback loop? Extra point for an example.*

Ecology & Land Management
- These are populations that produce more individuals than the area will support and can contribute to other populations through emigration – *What are source populations?*
- These populations do not produce enough individuals to support their own numbers and require immigration to sustain themselves – *What are sink populations?*
- Explain why climate change may prove problematic for the biological reserve method of protecting biodiversity (the idea of having nature reserves or national parks to protect biodiversity)? *While land can be protected, ecosystems are dynamic and ever changing. Climate change may alter a reserve's characteristics to a point where the habitat no longer supports the species being protected, thereby jeopardizing those species.*

This management tool is allowing conservation biologists to connect wildlife reserves so that organisms can breed and share genetic material as areas change through time – *What are wildlife corridors?*

Sustainability

- _____ & _____ are two examples of ecosystem services – *What are clean water, clean air, crop pollination, pest control, protection from extreme weather, protection from UV radiation, flood protection, cycling of nutrients, etc.*
- This simple concept still remains one of most important goals for reducing the impact humans have on Earth's living and non-living systems – *What is reduce human population growth?*
- What can we do in our own lives to reduce our ecological footprint on Earth? Have student teams make a list and then go from group to group getting one response each. Award points for each new answer to encourage students searching for creative answers. *(Ideas: reduce waste, reduce energy use, mend things, buy used stuff, buy wisely, use energy efficient products, use public transportation, walk and bike commute, buy food locally, reduce the amount of consumers you eat, avoid products with harmful chemicals, support small local businesses, build community where you live, etc.)*

ECOLOGICAL MAPPING ACTIVITY

This activity is a great follow-up activity after teaching some of the basic ecological concepts. You could also use it to introduce these concepts by having students complete the map first and then following up with some sharing about observations students made and the relationships, patterns, and processes they noticed.

Learning Objectives - The Learner Will Be Able to:

- Describe how living organisms are distributed across a three-dimensional landscape by mapping them.
- Graphically depict the concept of interconnectedness through mapping out the landscape.
- Creatively depict ecological processes, cycles, and patterns in a wilderness environment.

Mapping What You See

- Give each student a piece of paper that they can use to map an area.
- Choose an area with nice views where students can all spread out a little bit, sit, observe, and draw all that they see (and some of what they can't see too).
- Ask students to make a creative map that captures some of the following things:
  - A depiction of the landscape around them.
  - A depiction of how plants and animals are distributed on that landscape.
  - Depictions of processes that seem important here like photosynthesis, respiration, etc.
  - Depictions of cycles that seem relevant like water, nitrogen, and carbon.
  - Relationships between living organisms; between livings organisms and their non-living environment. Who's eating what, where are critters spending their time, etc.?
  - The flow of energy beginning with the sun and flowing through food webs.
  - Depictions of different relationships among organisms like predation, herbivores, competition, parasitism, commensalism, and mutualism.

They need not capture all of these, but emphasize that they should observe what they see (and don't see but understand is still there) and creatively convey this.

- Some students may wish to use writing to capture what they observe or a combination of pictures and writing. Allow student some flexibility in how they communicate what they see. Just emphasize that you want them to observe and think about connections and patterns.

Reflection

- After students have 30 minutes to an hour to sit, think, observe, and draw, bring the group back together to share.
- Have students briefly present what they observed and chose to depict in their maps.
- Ask students what thoughts they had as they were doing this activity. Allow room for all types of personal reflection that may have occurred.

Conclusion and Transfer of Learning

- Remind students that all of these things exist and happen everywhere, even in cities.
- Inspire students to take the time to "stop and smell the roses" when they're at home. Stop and look at what is going on around you and reflect on all the connections that exist between living and nonliving things and with us.
- This activity is a great way to incorporate/introduce/infuse "sense of place" into the environmental science curriculum.

CREATING CONSCIENTIOUS NATURE NUGGETS
By Andrew Weidmann

"Nature Nuggets" are commonly used teaching tools for both students and instructors on NOLS courses. They can be powerful educational tools for students as they promote leadership opportunities, evoke inquiry, and promote connection between people and their environment.

However, at times Nature Nuggets can be disconnected, tangential bits of information that folks have read and regurgitated from a course library. They do not directly weave information into greater ecological concepts, do not connect to their audiences, and do not promote long-term student understanding on the topics. How then do we instructors help piece together nuggets that are more meaningful in these critical arenas?

This piece is intended to offer tools to teach more conscientious nature nuggets for instructors and students. In addition, the article provides a model for students and instructors to approach teaching one another as well as an example Nature Nugget on nitrogen fixation.

Teaching Model

1) Anticipatory Set—Provide a "hook" for students to see the relevance of the learning to their lives. It also enables students to become receptive to learning the subject matter.
2) Learning Objectives— Identify specifically what the student will be able to do, understand, and/or care about as a result of the lesson.
3) Teaching—*Input:* The teacher provides the information needed for students to gain the knowledge or skill through lecture, skit, rap, etc. *Modeling:* The instructor illustrates application of the information (problem-solving, comparison, summarizing, etc.).

Checking for Understanding: Determine whether students have "got it" before proceeding. This typically involves asking to gauge level of comprehension.

4) Guided Practice—Provide an opportunity for each student to demonstrate comprehension by working through an activity or exercise under the instructor's supervision, helping students as needed.

5) Closure—Remind the students what the objectives were and what was taught. Further connect new concepts to the course's educational goals.

6) Independent Practice—Reinforce through repeated practice so that learning is not forgotten. These assessments should offer enough different contexts so that the skill/concept may be applied to many other relevant situations.

NITROGEN FIXATION NATURE NUGGET
by Andrew Weidmann

Anticipatory Set

What are DNA and protein for and why do we care about them? (Allow student brainstorming – possible answers include "DNA is the blueprint of life," or "Proteins build, maintain, and replace tissues in your body." Nitrogen is also a vital element in the pigment chlorophyll, which allows the capture of light energy to construct sugar in plants.) What is the most essential element in the building blocks of DNA, RNA, and Proteins? Answer – Nitrogen! This element composes nearly 4/5 of the atmosphere, but we cannot acquire it in the air we breathe. Plants also cannot acquire nitrogen from the atmosphere but must absorb it through their roots in the form of nitrates and ammonia. So how, do we get this essential element?

Learning Objectives - The Learner Will Be Able to:

• Identify three different ways that Nitrogen is "fixed" from its atmospheric (inorganic) form to its consumable (organic) form, these processes ultimately define the "nitrogen cycle."

• Conceptualize and identify nitrogen-fixating agents in their living worlds for the remainder of their lives.

• Weigh nitrogen fixation's influence in an ecosystem and critically reflect on how the actions of humans affect this balance.

Teaching

(With two student volunteers) Have students hug each other tightly. This strong, and affectionate, bond symbolizes two Nitrogen molecules (N2) fused together in atmospheric form. To be used by living things this bond must be broken, and is only accomplished with a large amount of energy. (With three more student volunteers) Student A – "Pele" provides the necessary bond breaking energy from strong naturally occurring forces – lightning, forest fires, and volcanoes. (Ask Student A for a volcano impression.) Student B – "Haber-Bosch," the bond is broken via anthropogenic processes as in industrially created nitrogen rich fertilizers (first developed by Haber-Bosch (Ask for an "industrial" impression)). Student C – "Billy B. Bacteria." Bacteria, most often near a plant's root system, can break bonds chemically. (Ask Billy for a "Bacteria" impression, good luck!)

Now have the bonded pair walk through this three-stage gauntlet. At each stage, the fixers will separate the bond between the two. Explain that the first stage (Pele), is the least frequent and lowest yielding of the three on the planet. The second stage (Harber-Bosch) gets a bit unorthodox. Here, humans have intentionally doubled the earth's

quantity of consumable, bond broken nitrogen on the planet via industrial processes. This has both positive and negative consequences.

Food yields resulting from nitrogen rich fertilizers have dramatically increased, thus promoting more stable, better nourished, and ever growing human populations. The world population has tripled since industrially created nitrogen rich fertilizers were created. Also, atmospheric carbon sequestration improves from the enhanced photosynthetic processes in nitrogen feeding plants, thus reducing a global warming trigger. Adversely, however, bond broken nitrogen has flooded well beyond many ecosystem's natural carrying capacity. Consequently, ecosystem acidification (a lethal agent), green house gas emission (via Nitrous Oxide (NO2) which is 300 times more powerful than CO2), ozone depletion (from Ammonia gas, NH3), and decreased species diversity—some plants thrive while others perish from an overflow of bond broken Nitrogen—all disrupt delicate natural balances.

Finally, the pair arrives at the third stage (Billy B. Bacteria). Here, the bond is broken chemically by a wide variety of nitrogen fixing bacteria. These bacteria are found in all ecosystems, and are an essential component to overall ecological health. They occur largely on the roots of plants in a mutually beneficial (symbiotic) relationship in which the plant receives fixed nitrogen in exchange for photosynthetic sugars. Other forms of soil bacteria also transform atmospheric nitrogen into nitrates through a series of chemical reactions.

A reverse process completed by another type of bacteria denitrifies nitrates (nitrogen in a form usable by plants) back to atmospheric nitrogen, thus completing the "full circle" of the nitrogen cycle. All volunteers sit down with a round of applause.

Guided Practice

Ask questions that probe for critical thinking. Some questions include:

• Which of these three methods do you think yields the greatest amount of fixed Nitrogen? *Bacterial fixation—although anthropogenic means are gaining ground quickly.*

• Why is Nitrogen fixation important to me? *It creates a consumable form of the element essential to build DNA, RNA, Proteins, etc.*

• Where does nitrogen fixation occur in our current wilderness ecosystem? *Blanketing the roots of nearly all plants (trees, shrubs, grasses, lichens, crypto biotic soil, etc.). Here, an instructor might pull a root sample from a local plant to show students. Also on the flanks of a bolt of lightening or the flames of a fire.*

• Where do we receive essential nitrogen in our field ration? *From the cells of every plant and animal we eat.*

Closure

Nitrogen is essential for all living organisms as it is a building block for DNA, RNA, and Proteins. It is "fixed" from an atmospheric (inorganic) form to consumable (organic) forms via natural combustion (Pele), anthropogenic processes (Harber-Bosch), and by bacteria (B. Bacteria). Nitrogen fixed industrially, particularly in fertilizers, has both positive and negative ecological consequences. Bacterial nitrogen fixation, often occurring in a plant's root system, is nature's mechanism for providing this essential ingredient.

Independent Practice

Answer (some or all) the following critical thinking questions in a journal entry:

- What impact, if any, are we imposing on naturally occurring nitrogen fixation in the wilderness we are traveling through currently?
- How do you weigh the adverse effects of anthropogenic nitrogen fixation on humanity's long list of environmental challenges? Do you think policy makers should offer it as much attention as, say, the climate crisis?
- What steps, if any, should we take to restore balance to the nitrogen cycle?

References

- http://www.newhorizons.org/spneeds/inclusion/teaching/march-and%20martella%20ausdemore.htm
- http://en.wikipedia.org/wiki/Nitrogen_fixation

CLIMATE AND WEATHER CLASS

Learning Objectives - The Learner Will Be Able to:

- Explain why air masses form and differ in moisture, temperature, and pressure.
- Explain the significance of water in moderating climate.
- Explain how terrain can impact weather and climate.
- Discuss and interpret weather maps with high and low pressure systems and weather fronts, then describe the weather associated with each pressure system.

Weather Versus Climate

Weather describes the surface conditions on earth in a given place at a given time while climate describes the average weather conditions over periods of time. While climate may change slowly, it does change: as the atmosphere changes, with changes in the solar system, changes in plate tectonics, and differing terrain, etc.

Concepts Impacting Climate

Understanding these concepts allows you to predict both climate and weather in a given area based on characteristics of that area (elevation, position relative to large bodies of water, terrain, etc.)

Air pressure decreases with elevation - Earth's gravity holds our atmosphere near its surface precluding it from hurtling into space. Air is denser closer to earth's surface because gravity is stronger there. It has higher pressure closer to the surface as well because overlying air presses or weighs down on it. The higher the elevation the lower the pressure.

Warm air rises while cold air sinks – Air molecules are in constant motion. Warm air has faster molecular motion than cold air and is less dense because it expands as it warms. Warm air will eventually cool as it rises, but initially its warmth makes it less dense so it rises.

Air temperature decreases as you go up in elevation – Air pressure and density decrease with increased elevation. Lower pressure means air molecules are more spread out, bump into each other less often and move slower. Temperature is the speed at which molecules move; slower is cooler while faster is warmer.

Water moderates climate – Water has a higher thermal capacity than land. This means that land will heat faster than water and then radiate heat to warm the air above it. It requires a lot of energy to heat water, but water can release a lot of energy as well. Large bodies of water can absorb a lot of heat and re-release it. Thus areas near large bodies of water will have moderate climates because the water is warmer than air in winter while in the summer it cools the air. Conversely, areas away from large bodies of water typically have large temperature extremes as the air is heated and cooled from day to night (think hot desert days with cold nights).

Land heats and cools faster than water, just like air – Land heats faster than water when the sun's energy hits it. Once warmed, the land then radiates heat back into the atmosphere where it warms air above it. Conversely, oceans absorb much of the sun's heat such that the air is generally cooler or more moderated near large bodies of water. That is why it is so hot in deserts during the day. The differential heating of air in different parts of the world creates different air masses and ultimately wind as they move around to establish balance. Remember, areas of high air pressure will naturally diffuse towards areas of low pressure.

Warm air holds more moisture than cold air – As warm air rises and cools, moisture will condense from a vapor state into water and fall as precipitation. This also explains why our skin gets so dry and flaky when it is cold (the air is very dry when its cold).

Mountains often cause upward movement of moist air, which then falls as rain (Orographic precipitation) – This is also known as the rain shadow effect, since the windward side of mountains will be wet while the leeward will be dry. Once the air passes over the mountains it drops in elevation, warms and can then hold more moisture and the precipitation ceases.

Let's Talk Regional Climate

Time to apply what we've just learned. Italics indicate correct response.

- Ask student's what the climate will be like in San Francisco during the summer? During the winter? *Mild due to water's ability to moderate climate.*
- What will the climate be like in Topeka, Kansas? *Hot days and cold nights, since there is so little moisture in the air and no bodies of water nearby to moderate climate.*
- What will the climate be like on the west side of the Cascade Range or the Southern Alps of New Zealand? *It'll be very wet with lush vegetation because the predominant weather pattern is fronts coming in from the west or northwest. As they hit the mountains and rise they drop precipitation. On the east side it will be much drier as the air drops in elevation and warms it can now hold more moisture.*
- Why is Seattle colder than San Francisco? *Seattle is at a higher latitude and the angle at which the sun strikes this part of earth is less direct. The light must also pass through a thicker portion of atmosphere, which reflects more of the sun's energy. It's not because it's further from the sun. While the distance is greater, it's not a significant enough increase relative to the total distance from the sun to make any real difference.*

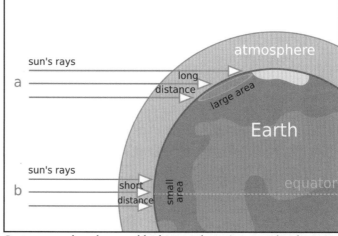

Regions near the poles are colder because the sun's rays are less direct and much of the sun's energy is deflected off the atmosphere.

- Why is it colder on Everest's summit than in Katmandu? *Remember, air cools at higher elevations because it's at a lower pressure and is therefore less dense, causing slower movement of air molecules, i.e., lower temperatures.*

Precipitation

Storms result when moist air rises to higher elevations where it cools resulting in precipitation. Warm air can hold more moisture than cool air and as you go up in elevation, air pressure decreases thereby resulting in lower temperatures. So, as warm air rises, it cools and condenses or sublimates to form rain and/or snow.

Air Masses

Certain areas on earth, like large oceans and large expanses of flat land, will develop air masses over them that take on the character (in terms of temperature and moisture) of the area. Air over large areas of warm water will tend to be warm and moist. Areas over large cold regions will tend to have cold air masses. These air masses move as a result of earth's rotation and wind currents. Once an air mass moves to a new place, it will change as it is impacted by new conditions of temperature, moisture, elevation (terrain), etc.

High-pressure systems result from cooler dry air masses that often form in polar regions. Layers of air pile on top of each other driving the air mass downward creating greater pressure with air that spirals outward at the bottom (clockwise in the northern hemisphere and counter clockwise in the southern hemisphere). They are also known as anticyclones. As the sinking air warms, moisture tends to evaporate (opposite of condense) creating good weather with no precipitation. They tend to be large and stable through time.

Low-pressure systems are associated with warmer moist air masses that typically form closer to the equator. Low-pressure systems have cyclonic air movement that is inward towards the center (counterclockwise in the northern hemisphere and clockwise in the southern hemisphere). Areas of low pressure result in rising air that condenses as it rises into cooler elevations and results in precipitation.

Causes of Precipitation

Fronts are the meeting of two air masses with different air pressure and temperature. These differing air masses form over different regions of the earth and move through the atmosphere as a result of pressure gradients and the earth's rotation.

Cold fronts form when a cold air mass slides underneath and pushes a warm air mass upward. They tend to be less dense and typically move fast resulting in sudden and short-lived rain and thunderstorms.

Warm fronts form when a warm air mass displaces a cold air mass upwards. They tend to be more dense and move slower - usually have stratiform clouds that bring increasing rainfall as the front approaches (often drizzly and foggy).

The orographic effect (relief rainfall) occurs when air is forced upward as it moves over mountains. The terrain simply pushes incoming air masses (Usually from the WSW in the Rocky Mountain region) upward. The moisture in the air cools and condenses resulting in precipitation. This phenomenon results in the windward side of mountains receiving most of the moisture, while the leeward side receives little. The leeward side is commonly referred to as being in the rain shadow.

Convective warming occurs as a result of differential heating of land surfaces. Land heats faster than water. Further, land without plant cover heats faster than plant covered areas and large landmasses like mountains may heat more than flat areas. As moist air moves over these areas of land later in the day after the sun has warmed

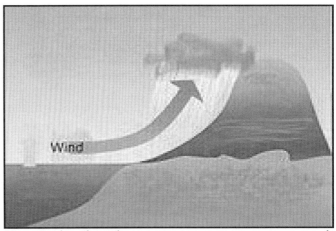

The orographic effect. When warm air masses encounter mountains, the air rises, cools, and condenses, oftentimes leading to precipitation on the windward side of the mountains. The leeward side is generally drier.

them, infrared heat radiating from the land warms the overlying air causing it to rise (convection). As the air rises, the water vapor in the air cools and condense to form precipitation. Mountain thunderstorms are commonly a result of convective warming as are tropical storms. At certain times of the year regular patterns may result in afternoon thunderstorms occurring consistently at the same time each day.

All three of these factors can interact in any given weather event. An incoming front may be further amplified by the orographic effect. Convective warming may also interact with a front to amplify movement of air upward resulting in precipitation.

Reading Weather Maps

Draw out a weather map and then interpret it along with the students.

- Regions of sinking air (colder air) are called highs, high-pressure regions, or anticyclones (they spin counter clockwise in the southern hemisphere and clockwise in the northern hemisphere). Clear skies and fair weather usually occur in these regions. Symbol: (H)
- Regions of rising air (warmer air) are called lows, low-pressure regions, depressions, or cyclones (they spin clockwise in the southern hemisphere and counterclockwise in the northern hemisphere). Clouds, rain, and strong winds often occur in these regions. Symbol: (L)
- The map on the next page shows a typical pattern of high and low-pressure regions. The curved numbered lines are called isobars. These pass through areas with the same air pressure in the same way that contour lines represent areas of the same elevation.
- Air pressure is measured in millibars. On this weather map the isobars are at 4 millibar intervals.
- The black arrows show the wind direction. High and low pressure regions do not stay in the same place. They move over the Earth's surface.
- The barbed line next to the L is a cold front. The barbs point in the direction the front is moving. In this example, the cold front is moving in an easterly direction.

Cloud Types

Simply put, low lying clouds typically result in precipitation. High clouds typically do not result in precipitation, but may indicate approaching "bad weather" (precipitation, wind, etc.). These examples

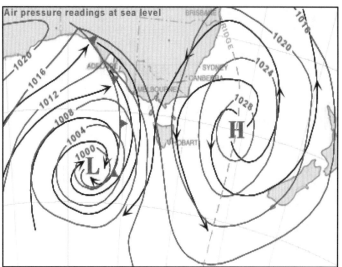

A simple weather map showing low (L) and high (H) pressure regions, wind direction, a ridge of high pressure (dotted line) and a cold front (barbed line).(Southern Hemisphere).

can serve as a helpful general guideline. Consider sharing the following bullet points. As you and the students learn and observe more, they're fun to point out when you see them.

- Typically high clouds like cirrus clouds may indicate incoming weather.
- A growing storm will show the clouds increasing and shifting to lower elevations (cirrus to cumulus).
- Typically, lower elevation clouds (they may still be tall as in the Cumulonimbus, a.k.a. thunderhead) are the ones that will precipitate moisture.
- The formation of tall clouds, like cumulonimbus, indicate convective warming and suggest the possibility of a thunderstorm.
- As a storm passes, the opposite cloud pattern can occur, as higher and higher clouds are seen on the trailing edge.

Conclusion and Transfer of Learning

- Understanding weather patterns allows us to plan ahead for trips, understand farming applications, etc.
- Different regions tend to have consistent patterns of weather that can be predicted based on their global location and terrain.
- There are direct correlations between an area's climate and the types of ecosystems that exist there.
- As climate evolves though time, so do weather patterns, and these changes impact both living and nonliving systems including humans.

GLACIOLOGY

Learning Objectives – The Learner Will Be Able to:

- Describe how glaciers form and move across landscapes.
- Identify parts of a glacier and landforms formed by glaciers.
- Apply knowledge of glaciers to locating crevasses.
- Name an impact humans are having on glaciers and how that change will affect humans.

Start by preparing a white board with a cross-section diagram of a glacier and, if possible, build a model of a glacier in the snow using rocks as the mountains. Begin with addressing the following questions, using the resources you've prepared.

What is a glacier? Large sheets of ice that flow like a river in response to gravity. They behave as fluids even though they appear "solid."

How do glaciers form? Continued snow deposition that doesn't completely melt during spring and summer changes through time as it thaws and freezes. It becomes névé (granular ice), then firn (ice somewhere between snow and glacial ice in density) as it becomes denser from overlaying layers. Eventually, glacier ice forms, which then begins to move due to gravity's downward pull or accumulated snow at the glaciers source (not all moving glaciers are flowing down slopes).

What types of glaciers are there? There are two main types of glaciers: alpine glaciers and continental glaciers.

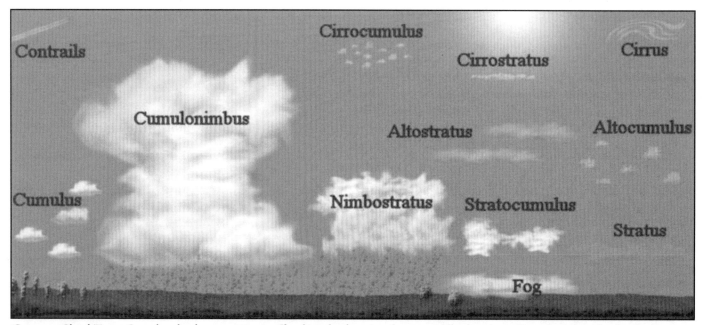

Common Cloud Types. Cumulus clouds are common puffy white clouds seen at low to middle elevations. Cumulonimbus clouds, also known as thunderheads, generate precipitation and can be the source of violent thunderstorms. Stratus clouds can cover the entire sky and bring long rainy days. Cirrus clouds are wispy and found high in the sky. Sometimes cirrus clouds are called 'mares tails' and can forecast incoming weather.

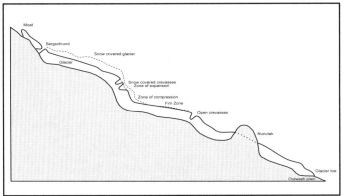

A cross-section of a glacier illustrating various features. A glacier slowly flows downhill, and as it moves, the forces affecting it create features like crevasses, bergschrunds, and moats.

Why is glacier ice blue? Ice is blue for the same reason the sky is blue (the Tyndall Effect). Just like water, it has a slight absorption of red light and reflects the blue wavelengths, not because O_2 bubbles in the ice scatter blue light.

Why are some glaciers growing while others are shrinking? Glaciers change through time as a result of the mass balance created by snow accumulation on one hand and ablation from glacier melt on the other. If a greater mass of ice is added from snow accumulation than is lost from glacier melt, then the glacier grows.

What are the parts of a glacier? Draw a longitudinal cross-section to show these: Accumulation zone: moat, snowfield, bergschrund, snow & névé, ice, snow bridge, icefall, crevasse; firn line; ablation zone: nunatak, moraine, outwash plain. I describe how the glacier moves across the underlying terrain and then explain how that terrain impacts the glacier. Rollovers tend to create crevasse fields as the glacier bends over them (like when you bend a candy bar and the chocolate cracks on one side and is compressed on the other side—a Snickers bar can be helpful to demonstrate this.)

What landforms are formed by glaciers? The best way to cover these is to build a model using some rocks and then snow. It is always great when you can point to some of these features around your camp, so plan ahead for this class: cirque lakes, tarns, moulins, moraines (lateral, medial, terminal), firn line, terminus, moraine lake, moat, col, u-shaped valleys.

Mapping Glaciers

If you are somewhere you can see glaciers, have students attempt to mark on a map where the glaciers actually are. Many maps depict glaciers larger than they are today given their trend of receding. Mapping them helps students visualize the change they've undergone over a certain amount of time.

Conclusion

- Choose an assortment of fun facts from the following list to share. Don't share them all at once.
- So what? How does this affect humans? What can we do to slow these changes?
- Connect this class to the ecological concept of "Change."

Glacier Facts

- Presently, 10% of earth's land area is covered with glaciers.
- Glaciers store about 75% of the world's freshwater.
- Glaciated areas cover over 5,791,532 square miles (15,000,000 square kilometers).

- Antarctic ice is over 2.6 miles (4,200 meters) thick in some areas.
- In the United States, glaciers cover over 28,957 square miles (75,000 square kilometers), with most of the glaciers located in Alaska.
- During the last Ice Age, glaciers covered 32% of the total land area.
- If all land ice melted, sea level would rise approximately 229 feet (70 meters) worldwide.
- Glacier ice crystals can grow to be as large as baseballs.
- The land underneath parts of the West Antarctic Ice Sheet may be up to 1.6 miles (2.5 kilometers) below sea level, due to the weight of the ice.
- North America's longest glacier is the Bering Glacier in Alaska, measuring 127 miles (204 kilometers) long.
- Glacial ice often appears blue when it has become very dense. Years of compression gradually make the ice denser over time, forcing out the tiny air pockets between crystals. When glacier ice becomes extremely dense, the ice absorbs all other colors in the spectrum and reflects primarily blue, which is what we see. When glacier ice is white, that usually means that there are many tiny air bubbles still in the ice.
- The Kutiah Glacier in Pakistan holds the record for the fastest glacial surge. In 1953, it raced more than 7.5 miles (12 kilometers) in three months, averaging about 367 feet (112 meters) per day!
- In Washington State alone, glaciers provide 470 billion gallons of water each summer.
- Antarctic ice shelves may calve icebergs that are over 50 miles (80 kilometers) long.
- The Antarctic ice sheet has been in existence for at least 40 million years.
- From the 17th century to the late 19th century, the world experienced a "Little Ice Age," when temperatures were consistently cool enough for significant glacier advances.
- Nearly all glaciers surveyed in Alaska are melting. Thinning rates in the last 5 to 7 years are more than twice those seen in previous years. Half of the water flowing into the oceans, globally, due to melting glaciers, is a result of melting in Alaska.

An overhead view illustrating the parts of a Glacier. As the glacier flows downhill its great mass carves through the surrounding terrain creating moraines, which are large mounds of earth piled up as if the glacier were a natural bulldozer. Much of the Rocky Mountains was carved by glaciers.

- The northern Andes contain the largest concentration of glaciers in the tropics, but these glaciers are receding rapidly and losses accelerated during the 1990s.
- Glacier melting has accelerated in the European Alps since 1980, and 10% to 20% of glacier ice in the Alps was lost in less than two decades. Half the volume of Europe's alpine glaciers has disappeared since 1850. By the end of this century, half of those left will have gone as well.
- Tropical glaciers in Africa have decreased in area by 60% to 70% on average since the early 1900s.
- The vast majority of all Himalayan glaciers have been retreating and thinning over the past 30 years, with accelerated losses over the last decade.
- The tropical glaciers in the Pacific have retreated, although in New Zealand some glaciers grew due to increased precipitation.
- Arctic glaciers have been receding, with the exception of Scandinavia and Iceland where increase in precipitation resulted in glacier growth. Greenland alone contains 12% of the world's ice; entire portions of the Greenland ice sheet appear to be sliding towards the sea.
- In Antarctica the center of the continent is currently cooling so it won't be melting soon. However, coastal glaciers and ice sheets in the Antarctic are melting. The melting of ice sheets and ice shelves that sit on top of land will result in higher sea levels.

Transfer of Learning
- The Earth is dynamic and changes over time. Glaciers have played a major role in forming the terrain features we see today.
- Humans may be altering climate in ways that are accelerating glacier melt. These changes are likely to profoundly impact human lives in the future (see "glacier facts").
- While humans may be impacting glacier melt, earth has been much warmer than it is now. One important question is have the changes occurred as quickly as they are now?
- While we see an overall trend of warming global temperatures, not all glaciers are receding. For example, some of New Zealand's western glaciers are actually growing as increased snow events are shifting the mass balance towards accumulation.

BOTANY FOR BEGINNERS

Learning Objectives – The Learner Will Be Able to:
- Identify the major plant groups and their evolutionary relationships.
- Define the role plants play in ecosystems.
- Identify the major parts of a flower that aid in identifying flowers and reveal adaptations.
- Dissect a chosen flower, illustrate it, and look up the flower in a plant guide.
- Describe the niche in which a chosen plant survives and reproduces.

Plant Evolution – A Brief Introduction
Most likely, land plants evolved from fresh water green algae, not salt water, around 450-470 mya. To make this shift, they had to adapt to dry, low density (air is less dense than water), temperature variable (water temperature varies less than air) and high oxygen environments.

The oldest record of land plants dates to 425 mya during the Silurian Period of the Paleozoic Era. It is now called *Cooksonia* and is a primitive spore bearing plant. It was a prostrate plant (lying low to the ground) with no leaves, flowers, seeds, or roots. Plants like this were likely the only land plants for millions of years.

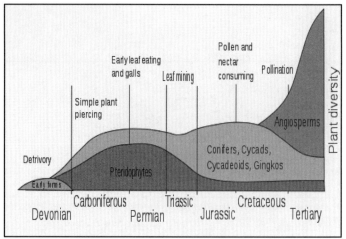

Plant Evolution. Plants have evolved and diversified over time, becoming more and more complex since their early forms.

The diagram "Plant Evolution" shows the evolutionary relationships between the major groups of land plants as well as the co-evolution of insects: "mosses" (early forms), ferns and their allies (Pteridophytes – first vascular plants), gymnosperms (first true seed plants: conifers, cycads, and ginkos), angiosperms (first true flowering plants). As the diagram depicts, most of our land plant diversity, now, is within the angiosperms (flowering plants).

The Role of Plants in Ecosystems
Plants photosynthesize and can convert water and carbon dioxide into sugar using the sun's energy. Furthermore, they release oxygen as a by-product of their photosynthesis. Plants in turn provide food to species that must eat other organisms to obtain their food, and provide habitat for many other animals, insects, birds etc.

Alpine plants may be an important indicator of changing climate, as they are sensitive to changing temperatures. The timing of snowmelt impacts when plants flower. Species will likely migrate up in elevation as annual temperature increase, resulting in some species going locally extinct as they have no place to go up on a mountain.

Flower Anatomy
The anatomy of a flower is only one portion of plant anatomy. Flowers are often the most common and definitive way to identify a plant. The diagram on the next page is of a typical flower. The vast variety that exists is a testament to how evolution can result in so many types of successful adaptations for different environments and relationships with other organisms (like pollinators).

The Role of a Flower
The function of a flower is to facilitate reproduction. Once the sperm from a pollen grain has fertilized an ovule, it matures into a seed within the fruit. The fruit is essentially the ovary, which may grow quite large. Fruits are adaptations for dispersing seeds. Many are edible and result in the swallowing of seeds by animals and birds that transport and then poop the seeds out somewhere else. Some seeds cannot germinate until they have passed through the digestive tract of an animal.

Flowers represent a wonderful example of co-evolution. Given the relationship between pollinators and flower reproduction, as one of these organisms change, so does the other. Some flowers are adapted to provide nectar for only one species of bird or insect. This means the bird or insect has no competition and that the pollen will most likely end up on another plant of the same species. In that way both species benefit from the relationship.

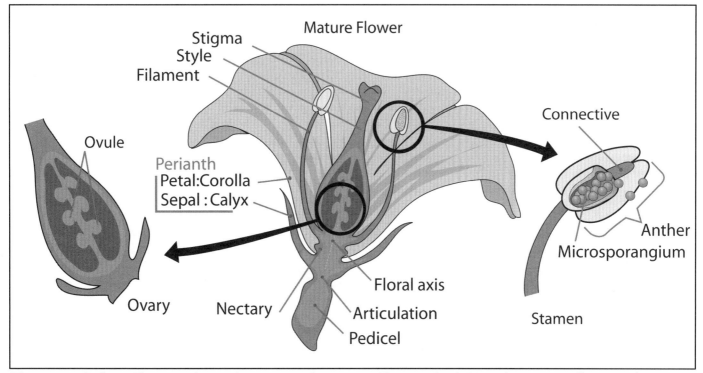

The anatomy of a flower. Flowers are the reproductive organs of angiosperms (flowering plants). Many plants require pollinators such as insects, birds, and bats to disperse their pollen to other individuals within their species in order to reproduce—an example of interconnectedness.

Collect Some Flowers

- Have students in groups of two go find a flower that they like. Have them sketch and diagram the flower with as many of the parts as they can. They may find that their flower is quite different from the diagram.
- Have them describe the type of environment that this flower was found in. Have them speculate what this flower must be adapted for. Are the flowers big and showy? Did they see any pollinators? Does it like wet or dry soil? Were any already in fruit?
- While students are working on this, pass around the flower book and see if students can find their flower. What else can they learn about it?
- Once students have had time to explore their flower, and hopefully look it up, have each group present what they found.
- Encourage curiosity even if you cannot figure out what a flower is called. Remind students that this does not mean they don't know what it is. Have them give it their own name. Every time they see it they will know what they call it. They'll know what habitat to expect to see it in.

Conclusion

- Plants play a crucial role in ecosystems as the only organisms that can absorb sunlight to create food. They in turn provide food to other organisms in the food web. All plants, just like animals, have a niche where they can survive and reproduce and they possess special adaptations to help them do this. Go around through your students groups and ask them to summarize their plants niche in a phrase, i.e., riparian area, montane forest, etc.
- Alpine plants may be especially sensitive to climate change as the timing of snowmelt impacts when they flower. They will likely shift up along elevational gradients as temperatures shift. This could result in local extinctions of many alpine species, as they have nowhere else to go up.

Transfer of Learning

- Learning about flowers can be very helpful in learning to grow your own food and in identifying local edible plants.
- Many of the plants we see in the field are in the same families as plants we buy at the store and eat, or that grow in our yards.

STREAM ECOLOGY
By Spencer Scheidt

Streams are perhaps one of the more overlooked ecosystems in the Rocky Mountains, but they are also invaluable resources that deserve careful management and attention. In addition, streams present educators with an easy opportunity to teach key scientific concepts in a fun and interactive manner. The ultimate goal of this class is to provide students with a *hands-on* opportunity to identify common organisms that live in streams and rivers and understand some of the basic precepts of stream ecology. Even if this is never taught as a formal class, the information presented here can be used as a resource for the suggested activities or sprinkled in as needed throughout the course and can be a helpful addition to the fly-fishing curriculum.

Learning Objectives – The Learner Will Be Able to:

- Identify common stream organisms and understand the environmental and biotic factors that structure their niches.
- Differentiate and identify different types of stream systems, and understand how these differences affect the stream organisms.
- Understand the impacts of human activity on streams.

Types of Streams

Streams can be classified in several different ways depending on the streambed rock type and the position of the stream relative to its headwaters. It is important to remember that mountain streams generally do not fall neatly into one category. These small differences can have large impacts on the organisms that can survive and propagate in these mountain ecosystems; be on the lookout for teachable moments or real-life examples throughout the course.

Streambed Classes

Bedrock streams have a solid rock bottom and offer very little nutrients, food, or protection to stream organisms. Only a few species of algae, nematodes, and mayflies can survive in such a habitat; different sets of species are specific to different bedrock types, so keep an eye out for changes.

Gravel or rubble streams are characterized by little sediment, high water velocity, and abundant (although hard to find) animal life. Mosses, algae, and diatoms combined with high oxygen allow the growth of many insect larvae (stoneflies, mayflies, and caddis flies), mollusks, amphibians, and trout.

Sandy streams are uncommon and unproductive; few plants, mosses, or algae can attach to the substrate, limiting the potential animal life (primarily nematodes and insect larvae) to the banks.

Silt and mud-bottomed streams have slow water flow, and thus accumulate large amounts of organic matter and sediment. This rich substrate, combined with sufficient sunlight allows high plant/algae growth, which supports a huge number of bacteria, protozoans, insect larvae, and fish (but not trout – ask students if they can imagine reasons why).

Stream Zones

Headwaters – Also known as brooks or crenal zones, headwater streams in the Rockies are generally fed by runoff and snow melt (occasionally springs), and are dominated by aquatic insects (constituting 95% of animal biomass). Organisms here often display adaptations to high water velocity.

Medium-sized streams – also known as the rhithral zone, these streams are characterized by cold, fast, oxygenated water. Most animals – including insects, mollusks, and trout - that live here are specifically adapted to these conditions, and are intolerant of warm water temperatures (which may become more common with climate change).

Rivers – also known as the potamal zone, true rivers are characterized by warmer temperatures, low turbulence, and higher sediment load. In slower stretches of a river, invertebrates exhibit many of the same adaptations used by organisms found in ponds and standing water.

Characteristics of Streams

Water Temperature – Due to the constant mixing of water in mountain streams, temperature is generally uniform throughout the water column. In general, both temperature and the range of temperature increase as you move downstream; headwaters are cold year-round, streams vary from 32-60 degrees Fahrenheit (0-16°C), and rivers can vary from 32-71 degrees Fahrenheit (0-22°C). Water temperature is influenced by the source of water (e.g. snow melt vs. runoff), the turbidity (cloudiness) of the water, and amount of shading by vegetation. Temperature structures species distributions, life cycles, and behavior. See if you can notice any changes in the composition of the stream community as your course gains and loses elevation.

Oxygen – In general, the more turbulent a mountain stream is, the more oxygen there is available in the water column. Often, headwater streams display higher turbulence than lower elevation streams (simply due to a higher land gradient), leading to high oxygen levels. Many stream organisms are adapted to nearly saturated oxygen levels, meaning they can be susceptible to eutrophication (nutrient pollution that results in low oxygen levels).

Flow – The rate of flow of a stream varies predictably with the land gradient over which it flows; steeper drainages have higher flow rates. However, nearly all stream organisms have at least some adaptations to deal with high velocity water (streamlining, grasping claws, suckers, deep roots, etc). Mountain streams often show irregular flow; rainstorms and snowmelt can periodically inundate streams, causing stressful conditions for stream life.

Available food – When plants and algae can handle the above conditions while capturing nutrients and sufficient sunlight, they fix energy for the higher trophic levels in the ecosystem. High production generally leads to high rates of consumption, more consumers, and more trophic levels. Can students observe or describe any food webs they observe in streams?

Types of Organisms

Stream life in the mountains can be easily grouped by their mode of feeding. However aquatic life is unique in that most organisms can alter their diet to fit whatever the water brings along.

Shredders consume large bits of organic material (plant or animal), and are generally found near headwaters. Examples include mayfly and stonefly Larvae.

Scrapers feed on algae and other organisms attached to the substrate, and are most prominent in areas of high production (middle reaches of streams). Examples include snails and caddisflies.

Gougers are specialized consumers of submerged wood and are abundant wherever there is wood to be found.

Collectors feed on fine particulate organic matter, and include the filter feeders; these are abundant everywhere, though they are perhaps most common in the lower reaches of streams. Examples include fly larvae and nematodes.

Predators are animals that capture and feed on other live animals, and exist in roughly equal relative abundance throughout the stream ecosystem.

Organism Identification

Pages 38-39 show some common examples of stream organisms that you may encounter on your course. While identifying species may be impossible, giving students the tools to at least identify the general type of insect or fish they keep seeing is an empowering experience that will help connect them to the landscape.

Human Impact on Streams

Even in remote wilderness areas, humans can still exert a large influence on mountain streams via local and global mechanisms. It is important to remember that these same freshwater streams serve as resources for human consumption – what we do to our mountain streams comes back to us, in one form or another.

Pollution - Whether industrial or organic, can play a large role in mountain stream systems. Mining waste in the Rocky Mountains lowers pH, increases sedimentation and introduces heavy metal toxins into many streams, killing or adversely affecting the entire food web. Organic pollution (primarily fertilizer from farming or eroded soil from logging) can cause blooms in primary production, but can result in eutrophication (nutrient loading), a process that can ultimately remove oxygen from a stream system as decomposers respirate when they consume excess algae. Stream organisms, particularly insects, are often good indicators of pollution; low species diversity or abundance could be the sign of upstream pollution. Be on the lookout for changes in species composition in areas with heavy logging and farming – these could be great teachable moments.

Stream regulation – In particular damming of creeks and rivers, can have large environmental effects. Not only are watersheds inundated by reservoirs, but alteration of the downstream flow of water can also impact stream life – fewer species of aquatic insects are found directly below dams.

Introduction of non-native species by humans can also dramatically change the composition of streams. In the Rockies, invasive bullfrogs and trout (especially rainbow and lake trout) have caused declines in native frog and salamander populations.

Climate change has the potential to alter stream ecosystems in several ways. Warmer temperatures may force stream organisms to change their distributions; alterations to the snow pack may increase or decrease discharge, or perhaps increase the irregularity of mountain stream flow. Changing conditions may allow the spread of invasive organisms as mountain habitat becomes more favorable to them.

Stream Nature Nuggets

These factoids may not fit directly into a formal curriculum, but they can serve the important purpose of stoking student interest, helping draw them into the scientific mind-frame, and establish connections with the land and life around them.

- One of the primary reasons rainbow trout were introduced to mountain streams to replace native cutthroats as sport fish was the fact that cutthroats were considered too easy to catch (fishermen may find this ironic).
- Trout can readily survive in streams and lakes that freeze over (but not all the way through); generally, enough aquatic insects remain active under the ice for them to not starve.
- Mayflies may spend almost a year as aquatic nymphs, but adults only live for 1-2 days.
- Some species of caddis flies are actually 'fishermen' themselves; while hiding in their houses of sticks or sand, some caddis larvae spin nets (up to 8 in long) to capture food particles washed downstream.
- Adult crane flies, also known as Mosquito Eaters or Hawks, only eat flower nectar, despite their fearsome size and appearance.
- Despite being known as the fire lizard, salamanders cannot survive temperatures over 100 degrees Fahrenheit (37.7 Degrees Celsius). Because they are so successful at surviving ground fires by burrowing into crevices and logs, they earned a reputation as fireproof.
- Toads have special parotoid glands behind their eyes that ooze a white viscous poison that deters predators – however, this fluid does not cause warts.
- Trout can alter the color of their camouflage to match that of their surroundings like chameleons, only much slower.
- Dead fish are good fertilizer – scientists have shown that decreases in salmon runs in the Pacific Northwest literally stunt tree growth (salmon are a primary source of nitrogen in the ecosystem)
- Fish have special sensory cells all over their bodies that "hear" splashes or detect the current. Trout use these cells to detect flies hitting the surface of the water.
- Just in case people believe species introductions were a thing of the past - in the 1980s, several "fishermen" introduced lake trout into Yellowstone Lake, decimating the native cutthroat.
- Sensitivity to mosquito bites is acquired – the first few times you're bitten by a particular mosquito species, you have no allergic reaction.
- Female mosquitoes drink human blood; they find people through the carbon dioxide they emit, along with several chemicals we release from our skin (incidentally, mosquitoes are not repelled by DEET until they land on you).
- Water striders hunt by watching for the shadows of water ripples on the stream bottom made by fallen insects.

Activities

These should be the heart of any attempt to teach the basics of stream ecology, as they are easy, fun, and informative.

Collect and Identify – Split students into small groups of two or three and instruct them to use their mosquito head nets to sweep through aquatic vegetation along the streambed. While making sure to keep the captured organisms submerged when possible, help students identify some of the common aquatic insect types with the help of this guide. Additionally:

- Turn over stones in the stream bed to find hidden stonefly and black fly larvae (carefully replace these).
- Look through stream-side vegetation for salamanders and amphibians; identify other predators such as trout when possible.
- After returning organisms to their respective habitats, informally discuss stream food webs and basic ecology.
- Get students to identify what type of stream they are observing – how do they think this affects what lives there?

Camouflage exercise – If possible, locate some caddisfly larvae that have built themselves homes out of sticks, rocks or sand. Using a set of tweezers, carefully remove the larvae's covering and place it in a calm stretch of water to observe how it re-camouflages itself. Additionally:

- Present different larvae with different options (sticks vs. rocks), to see if they have a preference. Which seems the most effective?
- Discuss with students why caddisflies may expend valuable energy creating such a covering. Which other stream organisms use camouflage?

Design a stream insect – Prior to collecting and identifying stream insects, instructors have the option of facilitating a discussion about the adaptations organisms have for living in fast moving water. Get students to draw their ideal aquatic insects on sheets of poster paper. Be sure to get them to portray body type (stream-lined or boxy?), feeding methods (fangs and claws, or nets?), camouflage, etc. Encourage creativity; some amount of silliness will make the activity more likely to engage students. Afterwards, be sure to complete the "Collect and Identify" activity and facilitate a discussion about how the real world adaptations students encountered compare to their imaginings.

Fishing and Stream Ecology – Fishing will offer students one of the most concrete ways to connect to the mountain stream environment, so take advantage of this opportunity to teach some ecological concepts.

- Trout gut analysis – After catching trout that students have decided they will cook and eat, carefully slice open the trout's stomach cavity to observe what it has been feeding on. See if students can identify what insects or prey were on the menu, and perhaps facilitate a discussion regarding food webs and interconnectivity – we eat the trout that eat the insects that eat the plants that fix light energy.
- When introducing fly-fishing to students, see if they can guess which flies are supposed to correspond to each insect. Highlight the amazing metamorphoses between nymph and adult insects, and discuss how fly-fishing mimics the natural behavior of stream insects to successfully catch trout.

Transfer of Learning

Stream ecosystems are great examples of how abiotic and biotic factors combine to structure the habitats that we see, e.g., the streambed type and water temperature determine what organisms can live where. Like all natural systems, streams are dependent on energy flow from primary producers to consumers.

Aquatic insect larva

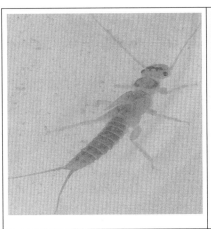 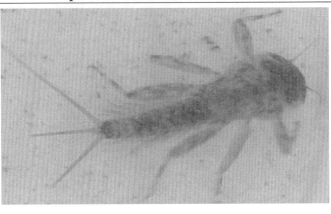 

Stonefly Larva	Mayfly Larva	Caddisfly Larva
• Two large antennae • Two tails	• Two short antennae • Three tails	• Live in houses of twigs, rocks or vegetation

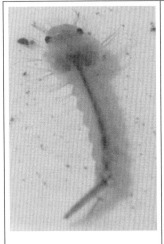 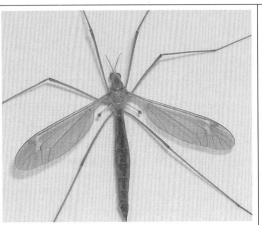 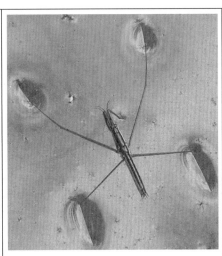

Mosquito Larva	Crane Fly	Adult Water Strider
• Float near surface to breathe; live in slow water	• Larvae found in cracks • Adult up to 3 in long	• 6 legs (true insect) • Middle leg hairs = rudder!

Amphibians

Tiger Salamander	Long Toed Salamander
• Can grow up to 1 foot long • Distinctive yellow to whitish spots	• Lives close to water sources • Characteristic long toes on back feet

Chorus Frogs	**Northern Leopard Frog**	**Western Toad**
• Bulbous throat pouch • Variable color	• Green/Brown with spots • Fully webbed toes	• Warty skin; sluggish • Lives in woods/meadows

Trout

Brook Trout	**Brown Trout**
• Distinctive dorsal worm-like pattern • Red spots with blue halos on sides • Common in small, cold streams	• Brownish gold coloration • Distinctive black and red lateral spots • Large trout (can exceed 5 lbs)

Cutthroat Trout	**Rainbow Trout**
• Distinctive reddish slash under jaw • Highly speckled, pink/brown in color • Native to cold streams and lakes	• Pinkish-red lateral streak, greenish back • Highly speckled • Common

Human actions alter streams, but we benefit enormously from the water, food sources, and natural beauty they provide. Mountain streams are great playgrounds for developing connection to and appreciation for the land. But remember, practicing LNT principles preserves them for future use.

References

- A Guide to the study of Freshwater Ecology, edited by William Andrews (1972)
- An Illustrated Guide to the Mountain Stream Insects of Colorado, by J.V. Ward and B.C. Kondratieff (1992)
- At the Water's Edge by Alan M. Cuancara (1989)
- Investigating Nature Through Outdoor Projects, by Vinson Brown (1983)
- Rocky Mountain Natural History, by Daniel Mathews (2003)
- The Great Rocky Mountain Factbook, by Susan Ewing (1999)
- Yellowstone Fish and Fishing, by F. Phillip Sharpe (1970)

ANIMAL TRACKING

Create a baseline for students so that they can begin looking for sign of animals and birds on their own. An accompanying tracking book will be very helpful as the example tracks in this lesson are very general to get you started.

Learning Objectives – The Learner Will Be Able to:

- Understand identification traits of some common animal tracks to the order and/or family level.
- Identify and interpret non-track observations to aid animal identification.
- Extrapolate the ecological relevance of the presence of specific animals within an ecosystem.

Track Formation

A very useful activity to start the animal tracking class involves having students walk around on an impressionable surface. Have students walk in a straight line on one pass, an S-curved walk on another, and then have them stop quickly, change in direction, etc. (be sure to not override theirs or others previous tracks). After students make these tracks, ask them to review the tracks, considering:

- How a simple walking track differs from a track made at higher speed?
- How changes in direction distort a track?
- How the medium traveled upon responds to differences in forces applied by the foot?

By focusing attention on the similarity and variability of tracks, students can gain insight into how tracking can sometimes be very straight forward, while at other times tracking can be a very compelling mystery. Moreover, developing a critical mind-set for analyzing tracks will enable students to engage tracking in a more nuanced manner than just memorizing tracks.

Track Nomenclature

Once tracks have been considered by students, a track nomenclature discussion can provide students with the technical tools needed to identify the basic shape and outlines of tracks. Look at a clear set of tracks (if possible) and discuss:

- **Length and Width**: Measurements made of the minimal outline as defined by the bottom of the track only.
- **Stride**: Distance from heel (or toe) of a foot to the heel (or toe) of the same foot where it next touches the ground.
- Straddle: Distance from outer edge of left track to outer edge of right track.
- **Group**: Distance from heel of first foot to touch ground to the toe of last foot to touch the ground. Used with gallops and bounding strides. Group length increases with speed.
- **Gait**: The type of movement an animal makes: trot, walk, lope or bound.
- **Digitigrade**: Prints made by walking on tips of toes, such as dogs, cats, and hoofed animals.
- **Plantigrade**: Walking on soles of the foot, such as bears and humans.

Walk like an Animal

Have students mimic the following gaits as you teach them. There are many variations for these. Dogs have a bounding gait, in addition to their alternating gate when they walk and trot, that creates a 3 and 1 pattern similar to the cantering gate of a horse. These basic gaits will get you started and are most common.

Non-track Animal Identification

While tracks are very useful for identifying animals, non-track clues can provide critical information that will help identify animals that left unclear or indistinct tracks. Non-track clues include:

Scat – The technical term for animal feces. Scat can provide information on the size and type of animal (refer to family characteristics for scat characteristics), as well as where the animal is traveling and living.

Animal Signs – Examples include deer browsing shrubs, porcupine chewed bark, digging, bird pellets, bones, small animals chewing on bones for minerals, urination and scratch markings by dogs, soil casts from voles and gophers during winter, rocks turned over by bears looking for moths, ungulates stripping bark from branches and trees while removing velvet from antlers, and food caches from Pikas.

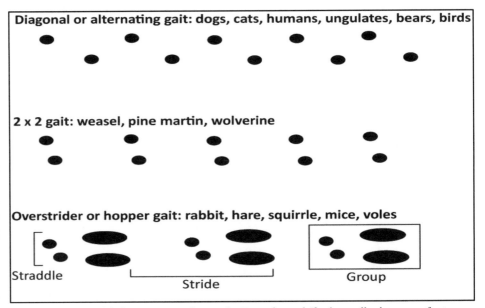

The varying gaits of different species of animals. Even if it is difficult to tell what type of print you are looking at, you may be able to identify the species by the pattern of the gait.

ROCKY MOUNTAIN ANIMAL TRACKS

Grizzly Bear	Black Bear	Mountain Lion	Red Fox
Bobcat	Grey Wolf	Wolverine	Coyote
Pronghorn	American Bison	Bighorn Sheep	Mountain Goat
Moose	Elk	Mule Deer	White Tailed Deer

The Relevance of Animal Identification

Understanding the role and interconnection between animals within an ecosystem can provide further incentive and depth to learn animal tracking. There is both value in becoming a good tracker as well as interpreting what the tracks tell the observer about the ecosystem they are living and traveling through. Expanding students awareness about ecosystem services and goods can arise out of informal or formal discussions about the role that animals play and provide within an ecosystem. This can tie into the ecosystem services concept by asking difficult questions such as:

- What value do animals provide to an ecosystem, if any?
- How do invasive species alter the value of animals in an ecosystem?
- Do animals need to provide a minimum amount of value to be protected?

Conclusion

Animal tracking is a great opportunity to develop both a sense of place through intricate observation of the natural world, as well as connect individuals with larger issues such as ecosystem services, biodiversity loss, and economic valuation of earth's resources. Care should be exercised in covering all of the information in this class—this resource provides a starting point from which to consider how to integrate animal tracking into an ES progression.

References

- Halfpenny, J. (1986). Field Guide to Mammal Tracking in Western North America. Boulder, USA: Johnson Books.
- Halfpenny, J. (1998). Scat and Tracks of the Rocky Mountains. Montana, USA: Falcon Books.

ASTRONOMY: CONSTELLATIONS IN THE SKY

Learning Objectives - The Learner Will Be Able to:

- Appreciate the night sky through exploring constellations and the immensity of the universe
- Identify a few common constellations and tell some of their mythology
- Differentiate between a planet and a star
- Use the North Star (Polaris) to determine which way is north
- Discuss the different types of stars (optional)

Choose an appropriate venue to explore the night sky with students—an "astrobivy" where everyone sleeps out together, or just a session of nighttime sky viewing. Have students share as many constellations as they know and then add in ones that you know. Share any mythology you know about the constellations. Some of the more common constellation myths are available through a website found under "references and resources."

Stars versus planets: The basic difference between a star and a planet is that a star emits light produced in its interior through fusion, whereas a planet only shines by reflecting light. So stars "twinkle" and planets don't. We can see 2,000 stars with the naked eye, with a radio telescope the number you can see is infinite.

Galaxies are clusters of stars. There are thousands of known galaxies each containing billions of stars. All the stars visible in the night sky are contained in our Galaxy, the Milky Way Galaxy. The Milky Way galaxy is shaped like a cookie (Barred Spiral). When we look at the Milky Way we are looking through it. It is called "path of ghosts" by the Vikings, "ashen path" by the Kalahari bushmen, "silver river" by the Chinese, and "bed of the Ganges" in Sanskrit. "The Milky Way" is of British Origin. The Andromeda Galaxy appears as a star with the naked eye but is more clearly a cluster of stars (sort of a fuzzy blob) when viewed through binoculars. Just as earth rotates around the sun and the sun moves within the Milky Way (our sun is moving toward the star Vega at 70,000 m.p.h.) our galaxy revolves 180 miles per second (1.2 million m.p.h.). So, earth's speed is 492,000 m.p.h. The Andromeda Galaxy is heading toward us at 168 miles per second. It is this outward expansion of the universe that leads scientists to the Big Bang Theory.

Constellations are groups of stars (which may or may not be actually close to each other) that ancient human cultures have named and associated with mythologies. There are 88 named and recognized constellations. Most of the mythological stories come from Greek mythology.

The North Star (Polaris) is the last star in the handle of the "Little Dipper" furthest from the scoop of the dipper. It is the closest star to the North Pole (about two thirds of a degree from it), which is the axis upon which earth rotates. For this reason, when you look at the North Star you are looking north and consequently it can be used for navigating as a known reference point. It is only visibly in the northern hemisphere.

Astrophysics (extra info to put life into perspective)

Hydrogen (1 proton & 1 electron in its most common form) and helium (2 protons, 2 neutrons & 2 electrons) are the simplest elements and comprise 99% of the universe's matter. All matter possesses gravity. Stars are born when a lot of hydrogen and helium are drawn together. The more matter, the greater the gravitational pull and ability to draw more hydrogen and helium. Eventually the gravitational forces are so great that hydrogen in the center (from the "weight" of the outer star) begins to "fuse" together in the center to form helium. This fusion reaction produces enough energy to prevent the star from collapsing in on itself and emits the electromagnetic energy we know from our sun.

Our sun has been stabilized like this for about 5 billion years and it converts 400 million tons of hydrogen into helium every second. 5-6 billion years from now, the hydrogen in the sun will have all converted to helium and the inward gravitational force will exceed the energy that previously prevented collapse. As collapse occurs, helium will fuse into carbon and oxygen and outer layers of hot hydrogen will expand forming a "Red Giant." This will likely consume Mercury, Venus and maybe Earth. Eventually the helium will all have burned up leaving carbon and oxygen. The mass in our sun is insufficient to allow further fusion, as in larger stars, and so it will progress to a White Dwarf and then cool to a Black Dwarf.

Novas occur in binary star systems (1/3 of all stars are in binary systems). As one star enters its Red Giant phase and starts spewing hydrogen, the other star flares up when the hydrogen interacts with it.

Large stars, twice the size of the sun, have gravity sufficient to fuse heavy elements (carbon and oxygen) resulting in the formation of iron and other heavier elements. The enormous gravitational forces of these stars result in faster fusion rates and shorter more violent life cycles. Eventually they implode, violently resulting in "Supernovas." All the heavy elements in the universe result from these stars and since earth is composed primarily of heavy elements (as are humans), we are truly made of stardust!

Very large stars, five times the size of the sun, are so massive that the inward gravitational forces exceed the outward forces from the fusion reaction explosions in the center, and so they collapse in on themselves. They collapse until they are a small point with gravitational pulls so great that even light cannot escape. Scientists call these "black holes" and are able to detect them.

Conclusion

- Ask students how you tell the difference between a star and a planet.
- Wrap up the activity by "quizzing" students to see if they remember some of the constellations they learned.

Transfer of learning

Stargazing is a wonderful activity that binds people together. Humans have stared into the heavens for thousands of years. We see the same stars as our ancestors. Ironically, the light from many of the stars we see left their stars before humans evolved and is just now reaching our eyes. This activity helps connect people with their surroundings and gain a stronger sense of place to some extent by dwarfing ourselves next to the immensity of the universe. The seasonality of constellations, or the differences between constellations visible in northern and southern hemispheres, can help students to reconnect with their NOLS experience in the future.

References and Resources
- A Field Guide to the Stars and Planets, by Donald Menzel and Jay Pasachoff
- http://www.laserglow.com/ and Amazon sell laser pointers that can help you and your students point out various constellation, planets and stars.
- It is recommended to print/download/learn several of the constellation stories from this website prior to going into the field http://www.comfychair.org/~cmbell/myth/myth.html
- http://spaceflight.nasa.gov/realdata/sightings/index.html helps you locate the International Space Station.

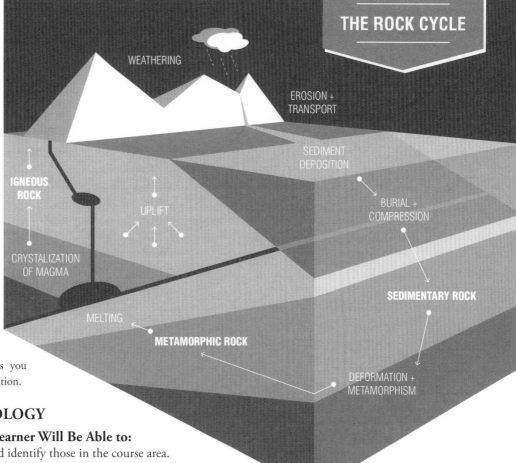

THE ROCK CYCLE

BASIC GEOLOGY

Learning Objectives – The Learner Will Be Able to:
- Name the three rock types and identify those in the course area.
- Describe how rocks and minerals move and change through the rock cycle.
- Find examples of and describe processes in the local geology impacting landforms (weathering, erosion, volcanism, glaciology, fault block mechanics, plate tectonics, etc.).
- Understand the connection between geology and other systems like ecosystems and climate systems.

In advance of this class, you'll need to put together some brief notes about your local geology. Keep it simple. Help students understand how long ago the formations around you began forming and ended forming, and then what processes and events weathered and eroded them to their current state.

The Rock Cycle
This cycle describes the transition of the three basic rock types:
- **Igneous** – Forms when molten rock crystallizes above or below ground.
- **Metamorphic** – Forms when other rock types are exposed to *heat and pressure* underground and the molecules are restructured into different rock types.
- **Sedimentary** – Forms as sediment is compressed and cemented together.

The cycle is driven predominantly by plate tectonics and the water cycle over long periods of geologic time. The following diagram describes the cycle and provides example rock types within each of the three categories. Recreate this diagram (you may simplify it for ease sake) in an interactive fashion allowing students to relate what many already know. Then identify the rock types you can see in your course area. Consider collecting some samples to hand out.

Three Processes Drive the Rock Cycle
Plate Tectonics refers to the large scale movement of the earth's lithosphere (hard outer layer including continental and oceanic crust) in the form of plates on top of the fluid-like asthenosphere, a layer in the upper mantle. Much geologic activity occurs near or at the plate boundaries.

Weathering refers to the process of how rocks are broken down into smaller pieces when they are exposed to the atmosphere. This can be both mechanical as water freezes in cracks and cleaves larger rocks into smaller ones, or chemical, as chemicals in air and water breakdown or dissolve rock.

Erosion refers to the process of transporting material once it has weathered. Water and ice are the major transporters of sediment via rivers and glaciers.

Mountain Building Processes
- *Fault-block Mountains* form as blocks lift and sink along existing or newly formed faults from tensional forces as the earth's crust is stretched. The Tetons and many of the Basin Range mountains in the Western U.S. serve as examples.

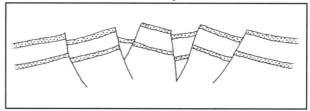

Strong tectonic forces put tensional stress on the landscape resulting in fault block mountains. The Tetons are an example of a tilted, or sloped, fault block mountain range.

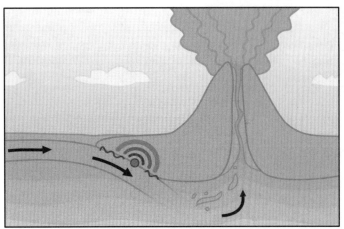

An example of a subduction zone. The oceanic plate always drops under the continental plate due to its greater density, and sometimes results in volcanism.

- Volcanism occurs where plates diverge (pull apart) as with mid oceanic ridges, or converge (come together, generally with one sub-ducting below the other) as with the Cascade Range. They may also occur from "Hot Spots" as with the Hawaiian Islands or Yellowstone.
- Uplift of the earth's crust occurs as a result of plate tectonic activity. Plates colliding may cause uplift as with the formation of the Himalayas, or one plate sub-ducting under another may result in uplift, with underlying igneous intrusions, as with portions of the Rocky Mountains.

Show and Tell

Once you have covered basic geology principles, take students on a show and tell. Pass around pieces of rock. Help get students to tell the "local story" of what happened here. Make observations about the formations around you. What are the weathering and erosional processes that formed them? What time periods do the rock layers you can observe represent?

Conclusion

Focus your conclusions on the "So what?" The following section on transfer of learning details the significance of geology and geologic processes to other systems. Have students come up with some of these on their own then choose a few others to share as well. Connect this class to the theme of "change," or ask students which ecological concept this class most clearly relates to.

Transfer of Learning

Fitting the changes the earth undergoes into the context of other systems is crucial. The following examples help detail the relevance of geologic change.

- Plate tectonics change the orientation and location of plates thereby impacting the climate. The distribution of species across the planet is also impacted by the collision and separation of continents allowing for species to migrate and then evolve independently upon separation. Where a plate is located on the earth, largely determines its climate and therefore the types of ecosystems that can thrive in those conditions. As plates move, ecosystems change.
- Much of the earth's carbon is stored as carbonate rock (like limestone). Chemical weathering of limestone dissolves it and releases carbon back to the atmosphere or into the oceans as CO_2, which can impact climate over time. Simultaneously, biological organ-

isms are secreting carbonates to form their outer shells, which ultimately settle to the ocean floor and may become limestone once again.
- Volcanism alters the atmosphere by inputting particulate that may reflect solar radiation and cause cooling. It also inputs CO_2 into the atmosphere influencing the greenhouse effect.
- Geologic formations play an important role in weather patterns as is clearly evident with the rain shadow effect on the leeward side of mountain ranges.
- Some electrical power comes from the transformation of geothermal heat underground into electrical energy.
- Metamorphic processes formed all of our fossil fuels after millions of years worth of solar energy stored in plant organic matter was transformed into oil and coal.

Assessment and Next Steps

- Geologic and landform observations make great entries in natural history journals.
- Take the opportunity to point out landforms and processes you see as you hike.
- Challenge students to illustrate the landscape during structured reflection time.

References

- Monroe, James S., and Reed Wicander. *The Changing Earth: Exploring Geology and Evolution.* 2nd ed. Belmont: Wadsworth Publishing Company, 1997

WINTER ECOLOGY – ADAPTATIONS FOR SURVIVING WINTER

Learning Objectives – The Learner Will Be Able to:

- Define the five forces that define a winter environment.
- Provide three examples of adaptations animals or plants have for surviving winter environments.
- Explain how natural selection drives the process of change to derive particular adaptations.

Evolution is the change in genetic material of a population of organisms from one generation to the next or simply changes in a population of organisms through multiple generations. Natural selection is the process through which individuals best adapted to their environment survive, pass on the traits to their offspring, and consequently result in populations that evolve. Remember individuals can't change; populations change as individuals with differing traits have differential survival. Winter environments are harsh and only organisms with well-suited adaptations can survive (compete for resources and reproduce). The following acronym summarizes the major forces in a winter environment.

S – snow – makes it hard to travel and access food.
C – cold – forces animals to conserve energy and acquire more calories to stay warm.
R – radiation – the form of heat loss resulting in much lost heat.
E – energy – difficult to acquire because there is less food and less thermal energy from the sun.
W – wind – results in lost heat from convection making it hard to stay warm.

Strategies for Survival

Physical strategies include changes in the phenotype or physical character of an organism to help it survive (thicker fur, more fat stores, traits that improve tasks in a winter environment (i.e., digging)).

Behavioral strategies include changes in an organisms day-to-day or seasonal behavior or life history that help it survive (migration, seeking shelter, forms or hibernation/torpor).

Conclusion and Transfer of Learning

Given what you've just learned, how would you answer the following questions:

- How will warming temperature trends as a result of climate change impact animals adapted to winter? Pika? Alpine flowers? Conifers?
- What challenges do seasonal migrations have on conservation efforts?
- How might snowmobile or ski tracks from tourism impact wildlife in a winter environment?

EPISTEMOLOGY AND SCIENCE (BACKGROUND NOTES FOR EDUCATORS)

By John Gookin, PhD

Students sometimes debate facts when the teacher believes the facts are clearly accepted as scientific "truth," but the student has a different system for ascertaining truth. For example, scientific journals have had little debate for a decade about whether the earth's climate is changing, yet climate change deniers use rebuttals that are not based on accepted science, but rather on politics and religion. We embrace scientific inquiry at NOLS, and we don't need to apologize for that nor give equal time to other world views. Epistemology is how we decide whether we believe information is valid or not and how we sort facts from opinions. The climate change issue is usually a conflict in epistemology, not science.

Principles of Inclusion

It is not okay to tell someone that the way they discern truth is wrong. Using the principles of inclusion, we should seek to understand the other culture—without judgment. But we can also politely explain that our school presents the scientific view of ecology, evolution, or any other science. This implies that we do not give equal time to creationism, which is a religious point of view and not accepted as science. Expect endless conflict if you try to use science and religion to disprove each other. There is a vocabulary of epistemology that helps us view it as a wide range of belief systems:

- *Opinions* are judgments that may lack clear facts. People should clarify that they are opinions and shouldn't try to disguise them as facts.
- *Faith* is our complete trust in a source. We should have more faith in information from peer reviewed scholarly journals than in information from entertainment magazines. Young people typically have more faith in authority figures like parents and teachers than older people do. Some people have faith in religious leaders, or in the Bible or Koran.
- *Dogma* is a set of principles laid down as indisputably true, e.g., some NOLS instructors who primarily work in cold environments can be dogmatic about not wearing cotton in the field, but this attitude is a disservice to students in hot climates. People with less personal experience, and less diverse experience, tend to be more dogmatic because they only know one context.

- *Intuition* is an immediate understanding of something without conscious reasoning. Conscious reasoning means that some decision-making factors are in your working memory as if you are discussing them with yourself. Experts have good intuition, by definition, because they have so much experience that they quickly use heuristics to make complicated choices. This expertise only applies within the area of deep experience and is not transferable, so an experienced brain surgeon shouldn't necessarily have good intuition about avalanches. The secondary definition of intuition is to use feelings more than rationale to reach a conclusion. When you are deciding whether to ski an avalanche slope and are considering the 128 factors we are supposed to analyze to decide how safe a slope is, pay attention to uneasy feelings because your mind can only keep about seven ideas in working memory at a time, but your subconscious alarm system might be trying to warn you that you aren't thinking of the right seven factors. Some people think intuition is like extra sensory perception (ESP), or other psychic abilities: this is referred to as parapsychology, which has generally not been shown to provide reproducible data, making it not an accepted science.
- *Hearsay* is unsubstantiated information heard from others. Rumors are information from undefined sources. Sometimes, instructors hear information a couple of times and start teaching it in their classes. But responsible teachers should question where information came from, whether it has been reviewed by experts, and the context in which it is relevant.

Conclusion

Scientific inquiry uses the scientific method to methodically generate reproducible data that supports or disproves theories that are often just hunches. Scientists generally publish their findings in journals that are reviewed by their peers, that is, the reviewers have expertise in that subject area. Upper tier journals have higher standards than the other journals. One scientist might "dis" another scientist by telling them they have opinions disguised as facts.

CHAPTER FOUR: SENSE OF PLACE

SENSE OF PLACE
By Garrett Hutson, PhD

Learning Objective
Students develop a sense of place by experiencing wilderness and exploring relationships with their surroundings.

There is a great deal of talk these days about saving the environment. We must, for the environment sustains our bodies. But as humans we also require support for our spirits, and this is what certain kinds of places provide. The catalyst that converts any physical location – any environment if you will – into a place, is the process of experiencing deeply. A place is a piece of the whole environment that has been claimed by feelings. Viewed simply as the life-support system, the Earth is an environment. Viewed as a resource that sustains our humanity, the Earth is a collection of places. We never speak, for example, of an environment we have known; it is always places we have known – and recall. We are homesick for places, we are reminded of places, it is the sounds and smells and sites of places which haunt us and against which we often measure our present.

(Gussow, 1983, p. 45)

Promoting a 'sense of place' in wilderness has consistently been a goal of NOLS courses and teaching practices. The sense of place concept has a long and rich history in the NOLS culture as an integrating idea that instructors use to empower students to develop meaningful and personal relationships to places we travel. For our students, we hope that a wilderness environment becomes a 'place' or a setting that becomes transformed into an environment of care (Tuan, 1977; Relph, 1976). On a NOLS course, a student's sense of place is felt on a personal level through the variety of meanings, emotions, and the experiential memories assigned to wilderness environments (Shostak, 2007).

Focusing on sense of place education at NOLS is perhaps more important now than ever before. Louv (2005) suggested today's generation of children are victims of *nature deficit disorder*, which impacts their perceptual and kinesthetic abilities to experience a sense of wonder in the out-of-doors. Louv posited that a sense of wonder is the root of spiritual development for children in natural settings. NOLS wilderness experiences are places for this sense of wonder to be encouraged, developed, and attached to students' capacities for life-long caring for the natural world. Consequently, NOLS instructors should not only engage students' sense of place during the courses they lead through a variety of approaches, but should strive to give NOLS students a variety of pathways to effectively nurture person-place relationships for the rest of their lives, regardless of where they live. Ideally, NOLS courses should be catalysts to life-long environmental ethics by providing students with personalized tools and approaches to reconnect with the power of 'place' any time they choose.

Empirical research studies related to the sense of place concept have shown promise in demonstrating relationships between pro-environmental behaviors and place-based sentiments (Walker & Chapman, 2003; Vaske & Korbin, 2001). In other words, the results from these studies suggest that as people develop emotional attachments to particular settings they become more likely to take action to care for those environments. Similar themes have been

intuitive within the NOLS culture for decades. Recent longitudinal research studies at NOLS identified five long-term outcomes for NOLS participants; two of these are an appreciation for nature and the ability to serve in a leadership role. It's important to the goals and outcomes of NOLS courses that leadership serves practical functions for students post NOLS. However, given that NOLS has not historically connected student appreciation of nature and development of leadership skills more holistically, it's now time to more intentionally challenge students to assume leadership roles in influencing responsible environmental behavior. This holistic approach to placed-based education connects sense of place more explicitly to the NOLS leadership curriculum and student experiences post NOLS.

The Purpose of This Chapter is to:
• Broaden conceptualizations of sense of place and its value for NOLS courses
• Present environmental studies at NOLS with 'place' as an over arching guiding concept
• Provide instructors with a toolbox for facilitating sense of place.

Finally, this chapter should also encourage instructors to think about their own connections to wild places and how they can integrate their own environmental sentiments into teaching practices making NOLS courses natural extensions of their passion for the natural world. It should be noted that the spirit of this chapter is not to provide or push a "one-size-fits-all" approach to sense of place. Rather, this chapter is meant to encourage continued dialogue around the concept of 'place' that will hopefully enrich NOLS experiences for all.

INSPIRING SENSE OF PLACE
By Garrett Hutson, PhD

How do students find meaning in places on NOLS courses? There is no single answer to this question; rather, there is an endless array of possibilities. Just like multiple ways of learning, people tend to find meaning in natural environments through their own personal senses, life experiences, and emotional reactions to different situations and environments. For example, after an epic day of hiking in the Wind River Mountains, I might sit with students while debriefing the day and be deeply drawn to the way the sunset changes the colors in the sky over mountain ridges. Another student may gravitate toward the details of the geologic history of the landscape, and yet another student may sense a special type of closeness to the group and the wilderness landscape becomes a backdrop for this relational meaning to unfold. There is no single pathway to place that is necessarily 'right' or 'wrong'. There are, however, multiple meanings that are attached to NOLS courses and to the environments where they take place. Tapping into the emotional realm of place-meanings can help to facilitate a sense of place for students. The concept map on the next page depicts examples of some of the different ways people attach meaning to places, as described through environmental psychology theory. The sense of place concept can be thought of as a combination of emotional, cognitive, behavioral, physical, and social elements. These elements coalesce in different ways to define one's sense of place. Potential debriefing questions have been provided for instructors to use casually or as a framework for more formal discussions on sense of place.

Note: Low and Altman discuss 'place attachment' in their work. The term 'place attachment' has been replaced with 'sense of place' for the purpose of this chapter.

NOLS students are drawn to places in a variety of ways, and may gravitate toward different parts of this framework. Different ways of sensing places can help students understand their own ways of connecting with wilderness environments during NOLS courses and after NOLS. Students should be asked frequently during NOLS experiences how they find meaning in wilderness places. Further lines of questioning are provided below that may help with this process.

Emotions: How do you feel in this place? Describe when you have felt the most connected to this place? What words would you use to describe the ways you feel about this place right now? What aspects of this place make you happy? Where do you find mystery in this place? When are you feeling distracted from this place? What parts of this place feel familiar?

Temporal: How does your sense of time affect you in this place? What aspects of this place remind you of other places experienced in your past that are special to you? What do you expect to learn from this place? (Ask at the beginning of a course) Describe what this place has taught you over time? (Ask at the end of a course).

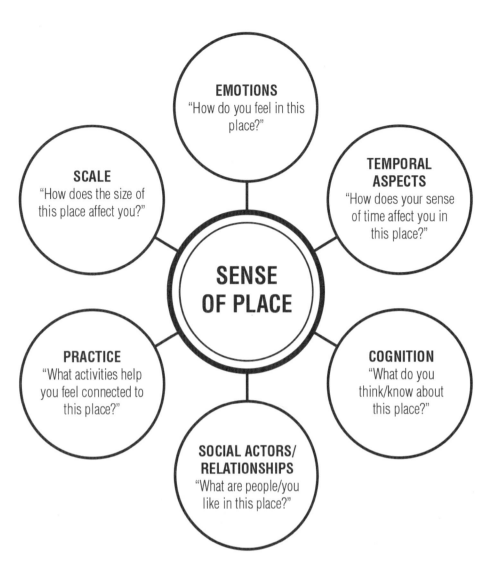

Sense of Place Chart (Low & Altman, 1992).

Cognition: What do you know/think about this place? What elements of the natural history of this place do you find most interesting or are you curious about? What elements of the cultural history of this place do you find most interesting or are you curious about? What patterns of weather have you observed in this place? What time does the sun rise and set in this place? How has the vegetation/landscape changed in this place during the course?

Social Actors/Relationships: What are people/you like in this place? How has the group influenced the way you interpret this place? How do you think this place has shaped group dynamics during this course? When do you feel at your best in this place? When do you feel at your worst in this place?

Practice: What activities help you feel connected to this place? What activities distract you from fully experiencing this place? What skills are you working on that you think might help you to more fully experience this place? What would you like to spend more time doing during your daily routine that might help you to fully experience this place?

Scale: How does the size of this place affect you? How do expanses of mountains/oceans/river valleys/glaciers make you feel in this place? How do the details of flowers/rocks/wildlife affect you in this place? What do you see as your environmental role/responsibility as a person dwelling in such an expansive wilderness? How will you continue to relate to such a vast wilderness after the course?

These types of questions can be built into formal and informal parts of NOLS experiences. Nightly discussions could integrate some of these ideas into the observations component of the popular ANCHOR (Appreciations, News, Concerns, Humor, Observations, Readings) acronym focusing on a different sense of place dimension each evening. Instructors can integrate sense of place discussions into student check-ins. This could range from in-depth discussions using the above line of questioning to simply asking a student, "How is your sense of place?" Or, "When have you felt the most connected to this environment?" Overall, inspiring sense of place should be used in concert with a student's individual experience. In some cases, sense of place may be engaged by reminding the homesick student to not take for granted that they are in a unique and beautiful setting that they may never experience again. For others, sense of place meanings may be deeply personal and rich interpretations of the wilderness landscape that transfer to environmental ethics that may extend well beyond the NOLS experience. The sample lesson plans on the following pages are meant to serve as practical tools for instructors to use to teach and encourage intentional sense of place awareness during NOLS experiences.

References

- Gussow, A. (1983). A sense of place. In S. Van Matre, & B. Weiler (Eds.), *The earth speaks* (p. 45). Institute for earth education.
- Louv, R. (2005). *Last child in the woods: Saving our children from nature-deficit disorder.* Chapel Hill, NC: Algonquin Books.
- Low, S. M., & Altman, I. (1992). Place attachment: a conceptual inquiry. In I. Altman, & S. M. Low (Eds.), *Place attachment* (pp. 1-12). New York: Plenum Press.
- Relph, E. (1976). *Place and placelessness.* London: Pion.
- Shostak, E. (2007, February). A field guide to sensing places. *National Outdoor Leadership School Staff Newsletter.* National Outdoor Leadership School.
- Tuan, Y.-F. (1977). *Space and place: The perspective of experience.* Minneapolis: University of Minnesota Press.
- Walker, G., & Chapman, J. R. (2003). Thinking like a park. The effects of sense of place perspective taking and empathy on pro-environmental intentions. *Journal of Park and Recreation Administration, 21*(4). 71-86.
- Vaske, J. J., & Korbin, K. C. (2001). Place attachment and environmentally responsible behavior. *Journal of Environmental Education, 32*(4), 16-21.

TEACHING SENSE OF PLACE
By Garrett Hutson, PhD

Sense of place is the relationship that develops between a person and her or his surrounding environment, that includes a combination of emotions, cognitions, and behavioral elements that are assigned to a particular setting and that provide personal meaning. For students, sense of place can be simply described as the ways they feel in relationship with specific parts of the natural world. Sense of place is most powerful at NOLS when an environment becomes a permanent fixture within one's life context and provides a reference point for current and future stewardship behaviors. Examples of sense of place expression during a NOLS course might include the following statements: "I feel at home in this place," "I am in awe of this place," "I am drawn to the rivers/mountains/meadows/smells/sounds of this place," "I will never forget this place." Students should be encouraged to think about, and give voice to, their own sense of place expressions throughout each and every NOLS experience.

Learning Objectives – The Learner Will Be Able to:
- Use all of the senses to experience outdoor environments.
- Realize that people interpret outdoor environments in a variety of ways.
- Understand that all ways of sensing places can be correct.
- Track their own place awareness throughout a NOLS course.
- Creatively experience and interact with outdoor environments.
- Use the senses to appreciate the natural world after NOLS.

Classes
The classes listed below provide a sample of experiences to intentionally promote sense of place during a NOLS course. These may be used together or individually depending on the course context and instructor team goals. However, it is recommended that I-teams introduce and familiarize students early on a NOLS courses with the many possibilities of using the senses to actively experience the natural world.

Sensory Circle – Enliven the Senses
Materials
- Artifacts native to the region (rocks, leaves, bone, water, bark)
- Bandannas or another type of blindfold for each student to use.

Procedure
Sit in a circle with students and ask for a few minutes of silence. During this time, ask students to take in the setting in their own way and to relax as much as possible. Guiding questions might include, "How do you feel in this place right now?" "What are you thinking about in this place right now?" "What do you know about this place right now?" "How does the air feel on your skin?" "What can you smell?" "What do you see that captures your attention?" This should be framed as an informal discussion, and student responses should not be judged by other students or instructors. A simple "thank you" from the instructor facilitating the activity is enough.

After everyone has had a chance to share, ask all students to put on their bandannas as blindfolds. Once students are blindfolded pass around one object at a time such as a rock or leaf. You might have another instructor assist with moving the object around the group. Have each student contribute a description of the object using one of the senses, making sure not to tell if they know what the object is (taste may or may not be appropriate for all objects – use discretion!). The point of the experience is to illuminate the variety of sensory responses unfolding within the group, not to immediately guess what the object is. The senses can be broadly defined to not only include seeing, hearing, touching, smelling, and tasting but should also include feelings, memories, thought processes, and insights (i.e., "The smell of this object reminds me of a rainstorm I got caught in last summer while climbing a mountain with my father"). Students may need to be reminded of all the different ways that places can be sensed. Repeat with all remaining objects time depending. After each object has gone around the circle, ask students to identify each object with blindfolds still on.

Debrief Questions
- What differences did you notice in your other senses now that you cannot see? (With blindfolds still on)
- What senses provided you with the most information? The least?
- How did other people's descriptions change the way you interpreted the objects?
- What do you notice or appreciate about this place now that is different than before the activity?

Transfer of Learning
- How does this place remind you of your home place?
- How might you take some of the sensory awareness you experience in this wilderness environment back home?
- What are some of your other favorite outdoor environments that you have visited? What are some of the similarities/differences in the ways you have sensed those other environments compared to this environment?

Conclusion
- Remind students to stay actively tuned into their sensory experiences within the environment during the course.
- Reiterate that there is not a wrong way to sensing place and encourage students to continue discussing what they are sensing and noticing within the natural environment during the course with other students and instructors.
- Remind students that the natural world is rich with different sensory stimuli, which can be experienced in different ways to enrich outdoor experiences.

Variations

- This activity could be used as a sensory introduction piece to a class on natural history, geography, or ecology.
- Use the senses as debrief questions with your group during travel days – "What did you hear today?" "What part of the natural world do you remember touching today?" How did you feel today traveling over that mountain pass?"

References

- Ford, P.M. (1983). *Eco-Acts: A manual for ecological activities.* University of Oregon.

A FOUNDATION FOR DEVELOPING SENSE OF PLACE
By Ryland Gardner, PhD

"A place is a piece of the whole environment that has been claimed by feelings."

- Alan Gussow

Learning Objectives - The Learner Will Be Able to:

- Facilitate an experience that allows the student to open up their senses to the wilderness that they are exploring on their course.
- Give students a foundation for gaining a greater sense of place throughout the course.
- Help students develop an initial set of skills that allows them to continue to nurture their connection with the natural world throughout the course and beyond.

Introduce the concept of developing a connection to a place. I often speak of the relationship that we currently have with the natural world and how we (westernized human culture) have created a situation in which we surround ourselves with human-made objects that decrease our day-to-day connection with the natural world. Help the students to understand that our species was once in intimate relationship with the natural world and that this connection is an inherent part of our wholeness as human beings.

Once students have an understanding of their inherent need to connect with wild places, have them sit quietly until you have given all of the instructions. Let them know that once the instructions are complete you will read a short quotation or a passage of your choice. Once the passage is finished, have them depart in silence to find a spot:

- Without speaking have students leave from the circle like spokes from a bicycle axle and find a place within hearing distance where they can sit comfortably in isolation (cannot see other students or instructor) for 20 minutes to an hour. As the instructor you will have to judge your students capacity for quiet reflection; I am often surprised by how much they enjoy sitting quietly.
- Once they have located a spot, have them sit and close their eyes. Once they have done this, they should take at least five deep breaths to help them relax into the place/activity.
- With eyes closed concentrate on each of their senses one at a time: smell, taste (how the air tastes when they inhale), touch (the sun on their face, the breeze on their skin, their body against a cold rock), and hearing. Have them do this for about five minutes for each sense (smell, taste, touch and hearing). After these four, have them open their eyes while focusing in a single direction (usually straight ahead) spending another five minutes integrating this final synergistic sense.

- Using a journal or notebook, have them write in a "stream of consciousness" flow for at least five minutes. Encourage students to let the feelings that they have been sensing flow from their senses out their fingers and onto the page without much mental processing. Let them know that it does not need to make sense.
- Once they have done this, have them sit quietly until they hear you call them in. Let them know that you would like them to return to you and reform the circle in silence.

Debrief

After all have returned, ask one-at-a-time about their experience; be very specific. Ask one or two to describe what they heard, ask one or two to describe what they smelled, and so on. When you ask about what they felt, be very specific to ask about what they felt physically with their sense of touch. Save their visual sense for last.

- Then ask them to describe an emotion that they sensed while sitting alone in silence. This can be quite powerful.
- At this point, ask if anyone wants to read what he or she has written. If no one does, I usually will read what I have written during this time. This usually helps to break the ice and then others will be willing to share. It is not a big deal if they do not but I have heard some amazing words.

When your debrief is complete, remind students that by doing this on a regular basis and recording their observations in their journal, it will help to nurture and deepen their sense of place.

References

- Abrahm, David (February 1997) *The Spell of the Sensous.* Vintage

THE ANDY GOLDSWORTHY NATURE SCULPTURE PROJECT
Adapted from a NOLS Staff Newsletter article by Eric Boggs

The Andy Goldsworthy (1990) project is an activity based on observations, reflections, and connections to place. It is meant to further those processes by allowing students to connect with the raw material that comprise a place, and make their own guesses about origin and processes, which have shaped them. The project's namesake, Andy Goldsworthy, seeks connection and understanding with his environment and does so by using nature as his pallet and canvas. He is known for creating sculptures out of raw materials of his natural surroundings including leaves, sticks, ice, clay, sand, stones, snow, and reeds. His captivatingly beautiful arrangements mimic natural patterns and are left among nature. He photographs each piece in his own form of time-lapse photography and revisits many of his sites throughout the seasons and records how his work has been altered by nature. He records the flow and dynamism of ecology and landscapes.

Materials

Artifacts native to the region (examples: rocks, leaves, bone, water, bark)

Procedure

The project is simple. Walk away from camp into an uncluttered area with students. Then start with a brief discussion of what it means to know a place. Ask students to conjure up places that they truly know on a personal level. Then give a personally inspiring quote about sense of place or ask a student to do so. Afterwards, introduce Goldsworthy through a few quotes. Brief students on risk management concerns (scorpions under rocks and no cliff side projects), discuss LNT guidelines and permit concerns. Then ask students to split up into groups and create their own nature sculptures. Give students 30 minutes to one hour for the activity. Examples might include images of the sun, personally meaningful symbols, animal sculptures, constellations, or anything else imaginable that students wish to create.

Then meet at a central location and begin the art show pretending to be snooty, eccentric, and bizarre art critics, and comment on each piece. Probe with a few questions about the origin, inspiration, and materials used. Also, encourage students to ask each other questions. Overall, this project has been met with unimagined success and student excitement. Students, like Goldsworthy, enjoy the freedom of just using their hands and "found" tools--a sharp stone, the quill of a feather, or thorns. They take the opportunities each day offers: if it is snowing, they work with snow; at leaf-fall, it will be with leaves; a blown-over tree may be presented as a work of art on its own. Students should be encouraged to stop at a place and pick up materials because they feel that there is something to be discovered. This is where they can learn to use their creative senses in place. At the end of the activity, remind students to leave the area as it was found and to replace all aspects of their creations.

Thanks to Ventura based Naturalists at Large (naturalistsatlarge. com) for this class concept. For images of Andy Goldsworthy's work check out his books, documentaries, or simply Google his images and laminate for class material. Enjoy stacking rocks, weaving stems, raking sand, and the simple joy that comes with creating. A few closing quotes from the artist.

> *"Movement, change, light, growth and decay are the lifeblood of nature, the energies that I try to tap through my work. I need the shock of touch, the resistance of place, materials and weather, the earth as my source. Nature is in a state of change and that change is the key to understanding. I want my art to be sensitive and alert to changes in material, season and weather. Each work grows, stays, and decays. Process and decay are implicit. Transience in my work reflects what I find in nature."*
>
> -Andy Goldsworthy

> *"Looking, touching, material, place, and form are all inseparable from the resulting work. It is difficult to say where one stops and another begins. The energy and space around a material are as important as the energy and space within. The weather, rain, sun, snow, hail, mist, calm is that external space made visible. When I touch a rock, I am touching and working the space around it. It is not independent of its surroundings, and the way it sits tells how it came to be there."*
>
> - Andy Goldsworthy

References

- Boggs, E. (May, 2005). Driftwood and stone. *National Outdoor Leadership School Staff Newsletter.* National Outdoor Leadership School.
- Goldsworthy, A. (1990). *Andy Goldsworthy: A collaboration with nature.* New York: H. N. Abrams.

ENVIRONMENTAL LITERACY
Garrett Hutson, PhD

The topic of environmental literacy has become increasingly popular in outdoor education theory and practice as an approach to fostering person-place relationships (Curthoys & Cuthbertson, 2002). Environmental literacy can be thought of as an approach to environmental studies, which exposes learners to being actively engaged with the multiple processes and histories of a particular setting (Stables & Bishop, 2001). Another way to think about environmental literacy is through envisioning the landscape as text. This activity will provide a framework for helping students to 'read' the text in the landscape in multiple ways.

Environmental literacy has been identified as functional, cultural, or critical (Stables, 1998). *Functional* literacy is one's ability to interpret objective information such as identifying and knowing the name of a particular tree and whether or not that tree is native to a distinct region. *Cultural* literacy focuses on human histories within a setting and the different roles of people at particular sites over time. *Critical* literacy is the ability of a person to define and understand their own relationship to a particular setting and to have the insight to recognize what practices and behaviors protect that relationship thus protecting the particular environment. The hiking day progression described in this activity is an interactive approach for students to teach about environmental literacy to inspire another way to think about and develop a sense of place (Hutson & Weber, 2008).

Materials

Note cards and background information on the wilderness environment you are traveling in.

Procedure

Instructors will want to prepare this activity ahead of time on note cards to be used in small groups during a typical NOLS travel day. Instructors should prepare 3-5 cards (or have students prepare these cards depending on the course type and age group) on each environmental literacy component – functional, cultural, and critical. These "nature nuggets" should be quick descriptors of the landscape that can be used easily when different parts of the environment are observed or encountered. In a Wind River Mountains context, examples could include, "White Bark Pines have needle packets of five, often contain squirrel middens underneath them, and grow at higher elevations in comparison to its relative, the Limber Pine" (Functional); "The Wind River Indian Reservation spans over 2 million acres and is home to thousands of Shoshone and Northern Arapaho Native Americans – Sacajawea, who traveled with Lewis and Clark, is buried near Fort Washakie, which is inside the Reservation" (Cultural); and, "There are drilling operations near Pinedale, which threaten a variety of plants and animals including the sage grouse and migrating mule deer" (Critical). Create enough cards for each student to deliver 3-5 nuggets during the day and the instructor should model delivering a card early in the day. Students may need some coaching to deliver their nuggets, but I often try to honor their own creativity and interpretation of the place, and encourage them to deliver the material however they choose. Sometimes, I like to create themes and do all 'functional' elements of the landscape one day, and then all cultural and critical on following days. Finally, I ask that students share what they've learned or found interesting during evening meetings so that all students are learning about environmental literacy from one another.

Debrief Questions

I like to bring the topic of the environmental literacy into small-group debrief discussions after a day of hiking. Questions might include the following:

- What elements of the landscape did you find most interesting? Functional? Cultural? Critical?
- What do you want to learn more about after making these initial discoveries?
- What are some ways the environmental literacy elements can be tied together? How do they affect one another? (Grazing policy is often a fun discussion to facilitate here if appropriate).

Transfer of Learning

- What parts of your home environment do you think of when you consider functional, cultural, and critical elements of the landscape?
- How has human history shaped the landscape you live in at home? How have functional and cultural elements changed in your home environment over time? What actions are being taken to be more critical of environmental degradation in your home environment? What sustainability initiatives exist in your home environment? How are you/will you be involved in these initiatives in the future?

Conclusion

- Remind students that sense of place can be nurtured and developed through different ways of 'reading' the landscape and encourage them to explore other stories that the environment holds during the course.
- Show students how being environmentally literate is connected to Leave No Trace practices. Environmental literacy can give students a context for integrating LNT practices into their lives after NOLS.
- Students should be encouraged to hold in their memories those moments where they felt the 'most' connected to the setting to help them make sense of environmental literacy on their own terms, while recognizing and valuing others' points of view within the functional-cultural-critical framework.

Variations

This activity is dependent on student "buy in" to the delivery and listening process. If it's not the right time to deliver this activity on your course, another option is to share the "nature nuggets" yourself, modeling enthusiasm for the material. However, if students can be empowered to deliver place-based knowledge, they will be much more likely to remember it.

References

- Curthoys, L. P., & Cuthbertson, B. (2002). Listening to the landscape: Interpretive planning for ecological literacy. *Canadian Journal of Environmental Education, 7*(2), 224-239.
- Hutson, G., & Weber, H. (2008). A day hike designed to promote environmental literacy. *Schole: A Journal of Leisure Studies and Recreation Education, 23,* 83-86.
- Stables, A. (1998). Environmental literacy: Functional, cultural, critical.
- SCAA guidelines. *Environmental Education Research, 4*(2), 155-164.
- Stables, A. & Bishop, K. (2001). Weak and strong conceptions of environmental literacy:
- Implications for environmental education. *Environmental Education Research, 7*(1), 89-97.
- Woods, R. (1994). *Walking the winds: A hiking and fishing guide to Wyoming's Wind River Range.* Jackson, WY: White Willow.

NATURAL HISTORY OBSERVATION JOURNALS

Many instructors choose to have students complete a journal during a course or semester section. As with all assignments, creating thoughtful, clear, and realistic expectations is key in setting up a valuable learning experience. Far too often, they can become a checklist where students rush to finish at the end. While some students will always take this approach, here are some guideline that might help you structure this learning tool.

Do's:

- Have students present at least one of their entries to the group. This validates the importance of your assignment and allows them to teach a bit. It also allows students to learn from each other's observations.
- Be clear about the types of things students might observe:
  - Plants and animals
  - Weather
  - Ecological processes they are observing or considering (some are hard to see). Have them relate these to their own lives, i.e., what role do they play in that process?
  - Discussions of environmental issues if the surroundings are somehow triggering that thinking. Emphasize observation.
- Give students a clear structure for what an entry looks like (ideally you should show an example). Have students include a drawing/illustration of what they see. Be clear that you are interested in their observations, not natural history from a book. Question prompts that help might be:
  - Where does this plant or animal live? Where did you see it (a clear description of your location, e.g., Deep lake in the Southern Wind Rivers near Haystack Mountain)?
  - A description of the environment that it lives in: wet/dry? Forested/alpine? Etc.?
  - What role do you think this plant or animal plays in the web of life?
  - What is the organism's niche? How does it compete for resources? How does it reproduce?
  - How does the ecological process work and what's your role in it?
  - Why do you think the plant or animal behaves the way it does?
- How long should an entry be? They need not be long, but I emphasize quality over quantity. Consider, requiring fewer entries but encourage thoughtful entries.
- Provide structured time in quality places for reflection and observation. Instead of having a class after a hiking day, meet and then have folks spread out. Require that they do two entries over the next hour. That still leaves plenty of time for other reflection. Most students will have higher quality observation time when you provide structured time where they are less distracted by tasks of the day.
- Tell students you'll evaluate their journals based upon their "level of effort." As always, not all students appreciate this type of activity. There should be other ways to evaluate them as well.
- Try to do at least one observation entry yourself to role model. Have students share their entries occasionally during an evening meeting and positively reinforce thoughtful entries. Share your own.
- Have a due date well before the end of the course and provide feedback before they are due.

Don'ts
- Don't just have students do a species list.
- Don't give the assignment and then not provide time for observation and writing.
- Don't give the assignment and then not have students share or read what they've written.
- Don't allow students to simply copy information out of a natural history guide.

Guidelines
Complete a journal with 6-10 entries (you determine the #) about things you observe in the environments we visit. Entries should include the following types of responses:
- Your location and a description of the environment (when relevant).
- Draw or illustrate what you see.
- What do you observe about the plant, animal, environment, process, weather, etc.
- What role does this plant, animal, process, weather play in the ecosystem?
- How does it reproduce? Access resources?
- Why does it exist where it does, or in the way it does? If you don't know, then speculate.
- Ecologically speaking, what is your connection to this thing? Think of as many links as possible.
- Can you learn anything else about it through natural history books?

SOUND MAP
By Marisol Sullivan

As humans we are highly sight-dependent. The goals of this activity is to help students listen to their surroundings instead of just "seeing" them, and to gain a broader awareness of the place they are living in and travelling through on their NOLS course. It is also a great opportunity to pause during a typically busy NOLS experience.

Students will need either a journal or a blank piece of paper and a writing utensil. Give students a quick introduction of the activity and then have them create their sound map in a location of their choice –preferably away from others.

In the middle of the page, draw a little circle (or an illustration of yourself). The blank page is the "map," and each student is in the middle of his or her "map." Have each student spend a few minutes listening to the sounds around them, and then write or draw in what they hear.

Sounds can include someone coughing or whistling, footsteps, wind, birds, a creek, etc. Encourage students to try and be really specific about where sounds originate in relation to their location, if they are loud or soft, if they move, what the quality of sound is, etc., and put this in as much detail as possible on their map, either in words with different "fonts" or with drawings.
(See "map" example below)

Conclusion
Conclude the activity in whatever amount of time seems appropriate (I usually give at least 20-30 minutes) and offer the opportunity for students to share either their map, their experience, or both.

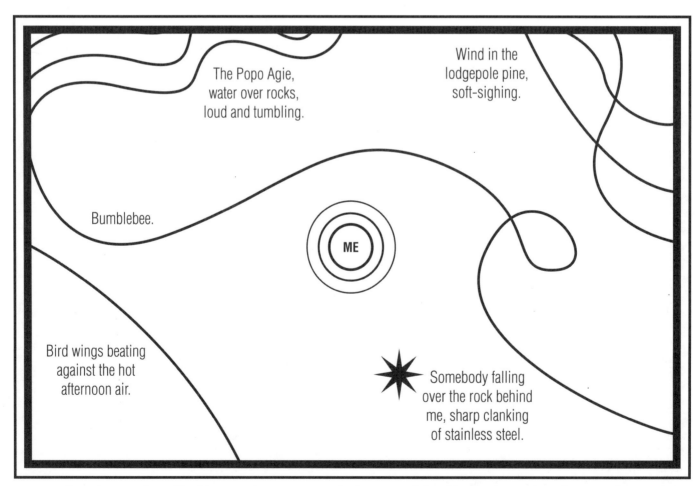

Drawing a sound map like this one can be a great way to develop a sense of place based on the sounds you hear around you.

CHAPTER FIVE: ETHICS

This chapter will help students understand relevant land management, policy, and environmental issues and how knowledge and ethics can guide decision-making for sustainable living.

We want each student on a NOLS course to experience, learn about, and connect with wilderness; this journey stands to influence their values. Then, we hope to challenge students to articulate how they hope to enact their own values into an environmental ethic. Their NOLS course will provide them with ample opportunity to practice their backcountry ethic as they apply Leave No Trace Principles while traveling in wilderness. But beyond this, our job is to challenge our students to transfer their values, and the ethics they are learning on their course, to their lives after NOLS.

The following articles and activities explore the meaning of values and ethics and provide ideas for how to engage students in a discovery of how they can enact their own values in their day-to-day lives.

EDUCATIONAL PROBLEMS AND DILEMMAS: IDENTIFYING AND NORMALIZING VALUE DISCUSSIONS
By Jesse Burns

As educators, NOLS instructors accept the responsibility, knowingly or not, of providing an unbiased education to our students. While the ideal of unbiased education has been identified in previous versions of the environmental educator notebook, developing a framework to implement unbiased education is a more significant challenge. As individuals, groups, a school, and an organization we possess values that, gone unchecked, could influence our ability to provide truly unbiased education for our students.

By identifying and normalizing (removing judgment about) our values as educators we can demonstrate to our students respectful, open, and clear communication about the NOLS curriculum. Ideally, students will be able to integrate their NOLS experience and learning into their lives with a clear understanding of how the values espoused on a NOLS course support, contradict, or are unrelated to their personal values. An exploration of values, problems, and dilemmas below seeks to identify the necessity and benefit of identifying the values upon which decisions, communications, and feelings are based.

Learning Objectives – The Learner Will Be Able to:
- Understand the difference between problems and dilemmas, and how values are inexorably linked within problems and dilemmas.
- Articulate how to promote engagement in environmental, social, and political issues in an unbiased manner.
- Gather information for facilitating productive conversations around value-laden topics.

Values
The Oxford English Dictionary defines values as "a person's principles or standards of behavior; one's judgment of what is important in life". The NOLS values of wilderness, education, leadership, safety, community and excellence are explicitly identified in all of our literature available to students. A recommended approach to starting a discussion about values would be sharing these values with students to open the door about value questions, such as:
- How do different people internalize each of these values?

- How strongly do we, as individuals and a group, hold on to these values?
- How does one respond to a value that they don't understand or believe in?
- What values can others identify as important within their life?
- What types of values (basic human values, social and political values, professional values, organizational values, personal values) do we all carry?

As an early tone-setter, such a discussion could make NOLS values explicit to students, identify that our values are not something that must be followed or believed in, and be clear that it is impossible to avoid being 'biased' due to the values one holds dearly. Rather, only by discussing these values can one become self-aware about their potential impact upon their actions. Developing the standard that values need to be externalized and/or analyzed in the context of their impact upon our interactions provides a clear connection to developing self-awareness and communication skills. Furthermore, identifying situations in which values *are* and/or *are not* central to a decision or communication can help our students further internalize the benefits of addressing values in an open manner.

Problems
A problem can be defined as, "a situation in which a gap is found between what *is* and what *ought to be*. To close the gap, obstacles must be overcome." (Cuban, 2001). Oftentimes, values impact the ability of students and instructors to recognize that the situation being dealt with has a technical fix, and that individual preferences (based upon values) are preventing a satisfactory decision from being reached. Overcoming a technical problem, while challenging, requires the problem to be identified and framed, which is where values can affect the process. Differing assumptions, experiences and positions can influence how a problem is framed, and the resultant solutions that seem plausible. As instructors, we have the opportunity to use these opportunities (e.g. route finding decisions, logistical decisions, etc.) to practice surfacing values in an atmosphere that is not highly charged or threatening, but nonetheless important and real.

Dilemmas
Unlike problems, dilemmas are, "…messy, complicated and conflict-filled situations that require undesirable choices between competing, highly prized values that cannot be simultaneously or fully satisfied" (Cuban, 2001). Many dilemmas arise on course (e.g. how to deal with a student who challenges us, how much ownership to pass off to students, helping students deal with conflicts, etc.), which provide wonderful opportunities to educate students. By normalizing the "highly prized values" we can respectfully approach conflicts, facilitating a process that recognizes the complexity of considering multiple strongly held values in coming to a decision. In doing so, we are providing our students with a perspective and approach that will enable them to address dilemmas throughout their life, rather than just giving them an 'answer' about what is the best way to deal with a situation. Instructors should try to model effective management of dilemmas, as a dilemma cannot be 'solved'. Rather, constraints (time, cultural & political assumptions, unclear expectations, etc.) lead to all choices feeling unattractive. Ultimately, a decision that satisfices* (Byron, 2004) should be facilitated by instructors (at least initially) as a model of how to manage competing

values. This provides an opportunity to differentiate between how different problems and dilemmas arise and are managed.

Satisfice—a utilitarian approach to making a decision that meets minimum requirements (satisfies) and requires all parties involved to sacrifice a belief or value to accept.

Student Engagement

Whether our students become stewards, active citizens, activists, or advocates, initiating a dialogue that connects our students learning about values, problems and dilemmas to real world issues is an appropriate next step. Current issues such as global warming, conservation, sustainability, development, and ecosystem services are examples of topics that contain both problems and dilemmas. For example, global warming could be mitigated with available technical fixes, but the variety of values held by many factions makes a technical fix unlikely. Instead, global warming is a dilemma that will involve satisficing, just as any local, regional or global dilemma will.

The role that students choose to embrace within and beyond NOLS, while interesting, should not be an explicit goal of our courses. While many students have become activists and advocates for the environment, there are many that have returned to positions that do fit into this category. As educators we could serve all of our students by modeling, teaching and coaching students to understand the importance of recognizing the role that values play within addressing problems and dilemmas. The numerous land management, public policy, environmental studies and leadership topics within our curriculum provide tangible opportunities to reflect upon one's own values, learn about other peoples values, and consider how one will or will not incorporate new values into their life. As educator's we should feel free to have a dialogue about how we, as one individual, manage this in our life. Helping students to achieve this high standard of conducting themselves as leaders could be one of the more lasting impacts of a NOLS education.

References

- Byron, M. (2004). *Satisficing and maximizing: Moral theorists on practical reason.* London: Cambridge University Press.
- Cuban, L. (2001). *How can I fix it? Finding solutions and managing dilemmas: An educator's roadmap.* New York: Teachers College Press.

ENVIRONMENTAL ETHICS (WITH THE LORAX)

By Trevor Deighton – Adapted by Jamie O'Donnell

Find a free copy of The Lorax at, http://ebookbrowsee.net/dr-seuss-the-lorax-pdf-d75803711

This class has been used by many at NOLS and proves to be a favorite with students. *The Lorax* by Dr. Seuss stands on its own as an inspiring story that makes us all pause and reflect on our behaviors. Many variations exist for this class. You should use the following ideas and suggestions as a guide to tailor the class to best fit your personality. Choosing an appropriate time when students are not exhausted and a location with beautiful scenery goes a long way in "setting the scene" for good reflection and thoughtful discussion.

Learning Objectives – The Learner Will Be Able to:

- Define and differentiate between values and ethics.
- Articulate what gaps exits between their own values and ethics.
- Discuss the metaphors from *The Lorax* and what real-world things correlate with the characters.
- Connect the story with moral principles that guide environmentally responsible behaviors.

Introductory Disclaimer to Students

Begin the class by stating that no one can be told what to value and how to act. Each of us must define these things for ourselves and enact our own ethics based on what we value. We can, however, inspire each other to recognize value in certain aspects of the world and impact people's ethics.

Optional Introduction (Where students get to share)

Say something like – "Each of us came here for different reasons, but the fact that we are all sitting here in this amazing wild place reveals that we value something about the natural world. Why do you value the natural world, places like this one, the environment? At some point in our own life there was some place, some experience, that we remember and to which we attribute our connection to the natural world (the environment)."

Now prepare the group for sharing some place from their life that they remember as being a special place where they felt connected to the natural world. Or some experience they recall that made them appreciate the environment and brought them to the present. Maybe it was a park they played in, a ditch, or a place they fished. Many people's place won't be very wild, that's okay. The point is it was meaningful to them; it taught them to value the environment.

Share your place first as an example. They'll mimic your style to some extent, so brevity but passion are good. Fifteen long stories takes too long, but every student should briefly share the place and why it was meaningful in establishing this connection for them.

Conclude the introduction with the take-home point that each of us values the environment because we've learned from experience how wonderful it can be. The greater our connection to the environment, the better we'll understand it, and the more likely we are to make wise decisions regarding how we interact with it. It is our responsibility to share with others what we have learned and provide experiences and share places with them that help them connect also. We only act wisely with something when we truly value it.

Introduction Continued

Either flow from the previous introduction or begin by defining a few terms. Throw the terms out to the group one at a time and let them share what they think each term means, then steer them towards a "final" working definition:

- What is a value? – The dictionary defines it as "the importance or preciousness of something." We can say for this class that a value is something that is important to you personally.
- What is an ethic? – The dictionary defines an ethic as a set of moral principles, especially ones relating to or affirming a specified form of conduct. In other words our ethics define our behaviors and we base them on a set of rules we create. In *Pavlov's Trout*, Paul Quinnett defines an ethic as "what you do in the dark before the game warden shows up."

Our values determine what we care about, and our ethics define how we act. Ask students to reflect on whether their values and ethics always align? Do their behaviors always reflect what they value? Of course, for all of us the reality is there often exists a gap between the two.

Briefly get students to share examples of the gap in which what they value about the environment or natural world is not reflected in how they actually behave on a day-to-day basis. You might have students list some of their values and then some of their behaviors. From this list, the group could then identify where the gaps exist. Make sure you're being humble and role modeling this as a personal challenge and reality for you as well! It is important to establish that if we truly value something, we must actively work toward enacting our values

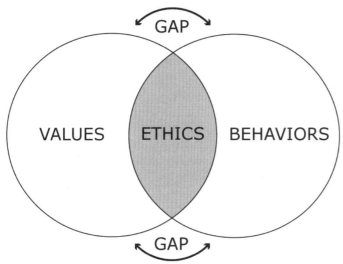

Ethics exist where values and behaviors overlap. This concept can be summarized as practicing what you preach. Your true ethics are exhibited by how you behave when no one else is around.

though our behaviors. It's one thing to say that we value old growth forests, and then another to consume wisely as to demonstrate that we will not support industries that don't share this value.

Consumerism Questions

Some instructors ask a series of questions that force students to reflect on consumerism, while some instructors do this after reading *The Lorax*. The order is up to your discretion. However, wait on facilitating a discussion. Just ask the questions and have students jot onto a scrap of paper the answers to the following questions. Add in some of your own that you prefer.

- How many pair of shoes do you own? Include all types including athletic/specialty shoes.
- How many drinks do you consume a week that are not water? Soda, coffee, tea, sports drinks, energy drinks, etc.
- How may "music listening devices" are in your current home? (Include those of other family members and roommates)
- How many jackets do you own?
- Choose other questions that highlight "thneeds."

Next, preface to students that you will read *The Lorax* by Dr. Seuss for two reasons. It is a story with numerous metaphors that highlight how humans often interact within our ecosystems (we'll discuss these metaphors at the story's end), and it is an inspiring story that reminds us of the importance of valuing the natural world and our intimate connections with it, as well as our potential to actually make wise choices and "do good." Now read *The Lorax* yourself or have the group members take turns. At the end ask students about the metaphors in the story.

Metaphors

Ask students what certain things from the story represent?

- **Truffula Trees** – These represent resources in our environment that can be bought and sold, e.g., lumber, mineral, oil, fish, land, etc.
- **Thneeds** – These are all the "things we think we need." They are made from resources we collect using energy we transform from other resources (often from non-renewable resources).
  - Now is the time to either ask the "Thneed questions" mentioned earlier or, if you already asked them, have students share their answers. This serves to remind us all that we consume far more than we truly need.

- Moral: We are all part of the problem. We all consume, but what we consume and how much we consume are personal choices that should reflect our values.
- Help students articulate what they need to survive. Use their NOLS course as an example of doing with less.
- Ask students whether they have felt happy and fulfilled on this course without so many of those thneeds? Wilderness living serves to teach us what really matters and what we can do without and still be happy.

- **Onceler** – Companies that produce products with finite life spans, using unsustainable processes and non-renewable resources. Who are the oncelers? Do we support any of them?
  - Moral: Be what Wendell Berry calls a "true materialist." Buy quality items, mend what you have, and waste as little as possible. Ask yourself, what are your thneeds?

- **The Lorax** – This is anyone who takes responsibility for educating the world on what's valuable in the environment and what responsible environmental behavior looks like.
  - Individuals that are mentors and role models like Rachel Carson, Edward Abby, or John Muir. Teachers, friends, and family; you could be a Lorax!
  - Environmental groups like the Sierra Club, The Nature Conservancy, or companies that strive to role model like Patagonia.

- **The Bar-ba-loots, swomee-swans, and humming fish** – These represent biodiversity and other ecosystem services like clean air, clean water, ecological functions that provide fertile soil through nutrient cycling, birds and insects that pollinate crops and wild plants. They have no monetary value as they are not bought and sold. Yet, we rely on them for our survival. When they degrade, there is cost to society in our health and well-being, but also to our pocketbooks. Environmental degradation costs society billions of dollars. These costs are external, though, and do not go directly to those degrading the resource and can highlight the "tragedy of the commons" concept.

Conclusion and Transfer of Learning

Spending time with nature teaches us its true value. To teach others we must remember what taught us, and share with them special places and experiences so that they will value the natural world too. We must work toward closing the gap between our ethics and our values. Recognizing what we need to survive and minimizing our thneeds takes us one step closer to living sustainably.

We must learn what healthy functioning ecosystems provide us, and better value these resources, as we depend on them. Change is difficult for all of us. Start small, but start. Reflect and challenge yourself first. Then strive to inspire others.

Assessment and Next Steps

- If students continue to be engaged, inspire a conversation about what we can do differently in our day-to-day lives to live more sustainably. Try to get students sharing, then fill in some of your ideas.
- Have students discuss in a journal entry what they value about the natural world, and how they will enact those values through a personal ethic. Have them address their own "gaps" and how they might overcome these gaps. Ask them to describe in what ways they hope their lives are sustainable in 20 years (if they value this). Will they commute by bike? Will they prioritize living close to their workplace? It all comes down to decisions, but envisioning what you want brings you one step closer to that reality.
- The "Lorax" can be found at the following link: http://ebook-browse.com/dr-seuss-the-lorax-pdf-d75803711

DEFINING ENVIRONMENTAL VALUES AND ETHICS: A JOURNAL PROMPT

Learning Objectives – The Learner Will Be Able to:

- Articulate what they value about the natural world
- Define a set of environmental ethics that reflect their values
- Set goals for the future that portray how their life will look as they enact their ethics

Defining exactly why we behave in certain ways proves challenging for all of us. Ethics are essentially our behaviors as they relate to a set or moral principles. What each of us values defines the foundation of how we behave, or at least we hope it does. And yet, we all make thousands of decisions every day, often without consciously connecting our behaviors to what we value. Consequently, only some of our behaviors are fully guided by what we value. Often, there remains a gap between some of our values and our behaviors. Reflecting on what we value and how we hope to behave increases our chances of closing this gap, in the same way that reflecting on our experiences helps us develop judgment.

After teaching Environmental Ethics, have students explore what they value about the natural world and their life through a journal entry or discussion. Remind students that sometimes our values conflict once they are put into action, i.e., practiced through our ethics. Recognizing where they conflict is an important exercise in decision-making. Also, have students define their environmental ethic. Frame this as their ideal ethic, or how they hope to behave in the future. This helps them identify goals for the future even though they may feel unable to achieve some of these behaviors in the present. Then ask, what are the challenges to enacting this ethic? Identifying the gaps between values and ethics is an important part in overcoming the common roadblocks we all face as we try to enact our ethics. Students should address the following questions (these are only suggestions, feel free to frame this in whatever way makes the most sense to you):

- What do you value about the natural world? Or, what environmental themes do you value (an example might be using only the resources you most need)?
- Describe the environmental ethic you would like to enact. Do this by describing what your life may look like in 10-15 years. What will you be doing, or not doing, that demonstrates living your environmental ethic?
- What are the roadblocks you imagine will prove challenging in always enacting your ethic, or what things might create a gap between your values and your behaviors?

Letter to Self

This activity may also be framed as a letter to self that serves to inspire students one year after their NOLS course. This may provide an opportunity to reflect on feelings students may have about "what's really important to them" while they're experiencing wilderness and what they would like to remind themselves one year from now. Research indicates that while a NOLS experience does influence responsible environmental behavior initially, behaviors tend to revert back to pre-course patterns through time. Sharing this with students may help bring greater meaning to this activity if they know that what they hope to enact when they return home may require some reminding down the road.

Conclusion

To efficiently conduct this activity and ensure that letters get sent, bring envelopes and have students self-address them. Then upon activity completion, collect the letters and envelopes and turn them in with the course paperwork or directly to your program supervisor.

CHAPTER SIX
POLICY, LAND MANAGEMENT, AND SUSTAINABILITY

Since 1965, NOLS has sought to teach people leadership and wilderness skills that serve people and the environment. Founder Paul Petzoldt strongly believed that people should travel in wilderness without destroying it. He testified before congress to support the Wilderness Act passed in 1964. Today, the wilderness we travel in during NOLS courses is not only our classroom, but, as we have learned, an intricate piece of the web of life. Ecology has taught us that all things are connected and that healthy intact ecosystems provide crucial services for humans. On a NOLS course we hope to continue to teach students how to travel in the backcountry with minimal impact as Paul initiated. We also want students to understand who manages our public lands on which we travel, and the inherent challenges land managers, government and the public have in balancing the multiple interests in how these lands are managed. But most importantly, we hope to inspire our students to act as leaders in their communities as environmental stewards.

As with all ideas, our perspective on public lands must evolve as we learn more. When Paul started NOLS, he recognized the importance of learning to travel in wilderness without harming it and to actively preserve wild places through legislation. At the time, these ideas were revolutionary. We know now that protecting land from development (as with Wilderness designation) does not necessarily protect ecosystems from degradation. We have learned that ecosystem processes permeate borders into and out of "preserved" lands. For this reason, we must strive to change not only our land management practices, but also our community and personal practices to minimize our impact of ecosystems. Decisions each of us make in our respective homes impact—positively or negatively—every corner of planet earth. Learning and embracing practices that are sustainable represents humanity's new challenge. Practices that tend to support nature's inherent ability to sustain life must not only guide how we manage public lands, but also the decisions each of us make on a daily basis in our homes.

The wilderness we travel through provides an inspirational classroom where we learn to appreciate wild places that have not been excessively altered by humans and intact ecosystems with a diversity of plants and animals. This opportunity inspires a connection between our students and place, and provides a leaping off point for defining their own leadership as decision-makers on earth. The following themes should be inspired during every NOLS course:

- Public lands managed by the government represent immensely important resources that provide numerous goods and services to people. Goods can be bought and sold, while services are more difficult to assign monetary value to. The challenge lies with how we balance the multiple, and sometimes competing, interests at stake.
- A combination of land management agencies and legislation define how our public lands are managed. As citizens of a democratic government, we assume a responsibility for electing representatives who will prioritize management interests in the order we believe to be most important. We also have the opportunity to guide the management process through numerous avenues of input.
- Humanity is faced with numerous challenges as a result of environmental degradation from human actions. These range from pollution to habitat destruction but ultimately result in diminishing ecosystems processes that support healthy functioning ecosystems. Given that we derive our goods and services from ecosystems, we are compromising our own future at the expense of our decisions today.
- Each of us makes numerous decisions every day that impact ecosystems, including those protected as Wilderness. As Aldo Leopold stated in his Land Ethic, "A thing is right when it tends to preserve the integrity, stability, and beauty of the biotic community. It is wrong when it tends otherwise." As members of the community of life, we must strive to make sustainable choices in our lives.
- In our 2013 Strategic Plan NOLS states, "Consistent with our mission, values, and strategic and operating goals, NOLS will work diligently to achieve greater sustainability in our use of natural resources. We will role model these changes to encourage our students and partners to adopt sustainable practices." While our impacts as an organization are undeniable, we are striving to reduce our ecological footprint and role model sustainable practices.

The following classes and activities serve to challenge students to understand what services ecosystems provide us, what environmental issues we face, how our public lands are managed, and what is at stake. And, how each of us participates as decision-makers. Students should learn about the agencies that manage our public lands and how they can influence those management practices. They should also explore their own impacts on ecosystems and explore how they can make decisions that support healthy functioning ecosystems. Discussions that highlight environmental problems can feel overwhelming, so focus your discussion around what we can do to enact positive change. Help students understand that not all problems have easy solutions, but that proactive efforts to live more sustainably are still crucial, even when they don't immediately solve a problem in its entirety. Our students benefit when we motivate through inspiration rather than intimidation. Many instructors have personal experiences they can share about how they attempt to live more sustainably that serve as a role model for students. We must help our students reflect on the experience they have on course and recognize the joys they feel while traveling and living simply, enjoying community, hard work, and the satisfaction of taking care of oneself and those around us. These experiences stand to inspire our students to act as leaders for living sustainably.

U.S. PUBLIC LAND MANAGEMENT

This class is best taught using examples of local management and environmental issues. Regionally specific public policy fact sheets, available on Rendezvous, will help you generate examples. There is more detail in this class than can be taught in one sitting, so pick and choose wisely and summarize points; additional information is included for your edification. This version of the class also incorporates some basic ecology and broadens the scope of impacts on our public lands to include personal decisions we all make on a day-to-day basis.

Learning Objectives - The Learner Will Be Able to:
- List the four main U.S. federal land management agencies, their missions and what branch of government directs them.
- Describe the role that major environmental policies play in public land management: Wilderness Act, Endangered Species Act, National Environmental Protection Act, Clean Air Act.

- Describe the various benefits we derive from public land, broadening this to include ecosystem services.
- Explain how their own decisions impact ecosystems on our public lands and the resulting challenges posed to a land preservation approach to conservation.

Ecological Concepts Discussion Points

Interconnectedness – all things are connected. Changes we make in our homes impact far away places, like the beautiful Wilderness areas we are traveling in now. Degradation to one aspect of an ecosystem will impact other aspects of that ecosystem. Also, ecosystems cannot exist in isolation. While setting aside land for protection is good, it alone cannot protect an ecosystem. What is going on around those ecosystems plays a role as well. Climate change caused by people all around the world is likely impacting this place right here, even though it may be federally protected.

Change – The world is always changing. Ecosystems are no different. While we want to "restore ecosystems" to a healthy state, going backwards is impossible. Some changes to ecosystems are irreparable. We must move forward attempting to promote healthy ecosystem functions, but along a new path in a changed ecosystem. An example is the introduction of non-native species. While we should attempt to control their numbers, some are here to stay. Pretending that they'll go away or that one day we will get rid of them may be an unrealistic and costly assumption.

Cycles – Cycle are an important part of healthy ecosystems. We must promote these by not damaging resources and species. Walking on cryptobiotic soils is an example of damaging an ecosystem component vital to cycling and providing nitrogen to that system. Aggressive resource extraction techniques have on occasion shown to damage soil ecosystems such that trees do not grow back like we might assume they would. This results in a non-renewable resource as a result of the damage that's done (at least over the short run).

Public Lands

Ask students what percentage of land in the US is public land? (32%) Explain that the public lands in the U.S. represent an important source of numerous resources and ecosystem services that we all benefit from. Briefly explain the mission of the four federal agencies that manage most of the federal public lands. Then have students help you place these agencies along a spectrum ranging from preservation to managing for use.

Other federal land management agencies include The Bureau of Reclamation, Depart of Defense, Army Corps of Engineers, Bureau of Indian Affairs and then most states have a system of state parks and some wildlife/game and fish department as well.

The Role of the Environmental Protection Agency (EPA)

The EPA was formed in 1970 to protect human health and to safeguard the natural environment—air, water, and land—upon which life depends. They play an important role in environmental policy and regulations, research, and education. The EPA does not directly manage public lands, but they may regulate actions that occur on public lands like the use of pesticides or allowable production of pollutants.

Multiple-Use

Some agencies manage for more than one use, sometimes creating conflicting interests among the numerous user groups. Have students generate a list of the way the USFS and BLM lands are used:
- Recreation (hiking, ORV, camping, RV'ing, hunting, fishing, ski areas)
- Range (grazing)
- Timber
- Watershed
- Fish and wildlife
- Mining (mineral and sub-surface resources)
- Energy (fossil fuels, natural gas, coal)
- Cultural resources

Ask students how these uses might conflict? What groups have interests in these uses? Which uses do we take advantage of?

US Forest Service (USFS)
- Founded in 1905
- Managed within the Department of Agriculture under the executive branch (historically because the USFS was harvesting trees)
- Mission is, "to achieve quality land management under the sustainable multiple-use management concept to meet the diverse needs of people."
- Manages 193 million acres

National Park Service (NPS)
- Founded in 1916
- Managed within the Department of the Interior under the executive branch
- Mission is, "to preserve unimpaired the natural and cultural resources and values of the national park system for the enjoyment, education, and inspiration of this and future generations."
- Manages 84.6 million acres

Bureau of Land Management (BLM)
- Founded in 1949
- Managed within the Department of the Interior under the executive branch
- The BLM manages 256 million acres, "for multiple resources and uses, including energy, minerals, timber, forage, recreation, wild horse and burro herds, fish and wildlife habitat, wilderness areas, and archaeological, paleontological, and historical sites."

US Fish and Wildlife Service (USFWS)
- Founded in 1956
- Managed within the Department of the Interior under the executive branch
- Mission is to work with others, "to conserve, protect and enhance fish, wildlife and plants and their habitats for the continuing benefit of the American people." They also play a role in management of species on other federal lands.
- Manage 93 million acres

The various land management agencies of the United States government that manage the majority of public land in the U.S. The BLM and Forest Service have missions that emphasize multiple use, and the Park Service and Fish and Wildlife Service put a greater emphasis on protection.

FEDERAL LANDS AND INDIAN RESERVATIONS

nationalatlas.gov™
Where We Are

The National Atlas of the United States of America®

U.S. Department of the Interior
U.S. Geological Survey

A map showing the public lands in the United States and the various agencies that manage the land. Where is the majority of our public land? And, what type of geograhpy predominates in those areas. Print a color copy of this map at: http://nationalatlas.gov/printable/images/pdf/fedlands/fedlands3.pdf

Ecosystem Services—What's Really at Stake

Ecosystem services are things provided by ecosystems that either directly or indirectly benefit human endeavors. These services include maintaining biodiversity, providing clean air and water, pollinating crops, moderating weather extremes and their impacts, dispersing seeds, mitigating drought and flood (wetlands), protecting us from the sun's harmful UV rays, cycling and storing nutrients, detoxifying and decomposing waste, and many more. While the public land agencies do not specifically manage for ecosystem services, we still benefit from natural services these lands provide. We are also impacted negatively when public lands are degraded and ecosystem services are diminished. Healthy functioning ecosystems maintain biological diversity at all levels (the genetic, individual, and ecosystem level). Functioning ecosystems that have diversity provide a myriad of ecosystem services that we require for our survival and are essentially free. Few of these services can be bought or sold, and yet their reduction would cost trillions of dollars to mitigate. In this way, degradation of our public lands represents a "tragedy of the commons."

Actions detrimental to ecosystem functioning

- Some forms of resource extraction (poor forestry practices, mining, energy developments, over harvesting of wildlife, fish, and plants)
- Over grazing
- Over-harvesting of water
- Inputs of pollution, toxins, and nutrients (we all contribute to these actions)
- Human actions that contribute to climate change (we all contribute to these actions)
- Altered disturbance regimes like fire and flooding that play natural roles in ecosystem functioning
- Introduction of non-native species
- Some development projects

Actions that support ecosystem functioning

- Different forms of ecological restoration – planting native species, removing non-natives, restoring natural waterways that have been altered, or removing dams that alter hydrology and wildlife
- Regulating hunting effectively
- Educating people
- Sharing our public lands with people so they might care
- Establishing sustainable ways of obtaining natural resources that protect ecosystem functions
- Decrease our inputs that increase climate change
- Simplify our lives and use resources wisely (reducing our consumption of goods and energy)

Protective Public Policies

Wilderness Act of 1964 – Since this act was enacted, over 109 million acres have been designated. "A wilderness, in contrast with those areas where man and his own works dominate the landscape, is hereby recognized as an area where the earth and its community of life are untrammeled by man, where man himself is a visitor who does not remain." The purpose of designated Wilderness areas is, "to assure that an increasing population, accompanied by expanding settlement and growing mechanization... has a system to be composed of federally owned areas designated by Congress as "wilderness areas", to be administered for the use and enjoyment of the American people in such manner as will leave them unimpaired for future use as wilderness." Wilderness areas can exist within any of the land management agencies.

Endangered Species Act of 1973 – Provides "for the conservation of ecosystems upon which threatened and endangered species of fish, wildlife, and plants depend." The act requires any federal agency to ensure that any "action authorized, funded or carried out by them is not likely to jeopardize the continued existence of listed species or modify their critical habitat."

National Environmental Protection Act of 1970 (NEPA) – This act mandates that any federal agency prepare Environmental Assessments (EA's) and Environmental Impact Statements (EIS's) for any proposed action on federal lands (drilling, cutting, building, extracting, etc.). The act does not apply to Congress, the courts, or the President. The act also provides opportunities for public comment periods and agencies are required to include these comments in their documents. Many non-profit organizations monitor the actions of federal agencies and comment on these actions on behalf of their interested members.

Ways to Protect Healthy Public Lands

- Realize that all things are connected. We cannot "build a fence around our public lands," and expect them to remain safe and healthy functioning ecosystems. Even designated Wilderness can be threatened from outside influences like pollution, climate change, and invasive species. The decisions each of us make impact ecosystems all across the world.
- Vote – all the land management agencies fall under the umbrella of the executive branch. This means that the president and his/her cabinet have a great deal of power in determining management priorities. Changes in office commonly result in dramatic shifts in land management.
- Learn about the issues facing public lands near you or lands you like to visit. Join organizations that monitor projects on those lands and contribute to support and voice in favor of what you believe. Projects are very much influenced by comments from the public to the agency.

- Call your representative and local policy makers when bills or policy are up for vote. It is their job to listen to their constituents even when they disagree. If you can't call, write a letter.
- Visit your public lands and see what and where projects are occurring. Nothing is more poignant than seeing a timber sale marked for harvest. You may find you are satisfied with their methods, or you might find you are appalled.

Conclusion

Ask students to reflect on where they live and jot down what they know about the public lands around them. Which agencies manage them? What are some of the common issues that arise in managing these lands? Try to get everyone to share briefly something about their homes.

Remind students that we play a role, even when we think we are not. Our choices on how to live, and our participation as citizens (or choice to not participate) impact our public lands.

References

- S. Naeem, F.S. Chapin III, R. Costanza, Paul R. Ehrlich, Frank B. Golley, David U. Hooper, J.H. Lawton, Robert V. O'Neill, Harold A. Mooney, Osvaldo E. Sala, Amy J. Symstad, and David Tilman, 1999. Biodiversity and Ecosystem Functioning: Maintaining Natural Life Support Processes, *Issues in Ecology*, Ecological Society of America, Issue 4, fall.
- Bureau of Land Management – http://www.blm.gov/wo/st/en/info/About_BLM.html
- National Park Service – http://www.nps.gov/aboutus
- U.S. Fish and Wildlife Service – http://www.fws.gov/
- U.S. Forest Service – http://www.fs.fed.us/
- Environmental Protection Agency – http://www.epa.gov/
- National Environmental Protection Act - www.nepa.gov/
- Endangered Species Act – http://www.fws.gov/laws/lawsdigest/ESACT.html
- Wilderness Act – at Wilderness.net - http://www.wilderness.net/index.cfm?fuse=NWPS&sec=legisAct

ECOLOGICAL FOOTPRINT CLASS

Learning Objectives – The Learner Will Be Able to:

- Explain what an ecological footprint is.
- Accept and understand that reducing their footprint by a little is better than none (i.e., help prevent students from feeling overwhelmed).
- Discuss lifestyle alternatives that allow for reducing their footprint with positive steps through collaborative efforts with friends, family, and community.
- Discuss the role the United States plays in resource use based on the average US footprint.

Ecological Footprint

What is an ecological footprint? Ask student what an ecological footprint is. And, establish a good working definition within the group.

How much land do you require to produce the resources you use? Have students brainstorm how many acres of land they require to produce the resources they use (help them conceive what an acre is i.e. slightly less than a football field). How many do most Americans require? What's the average footprint on an international level? How do other countries rank compared to us? For each of these questions have students share their guess but don't share the stats just yet. Let's build a bit of anticipation.

Ecological Footprint Chart (1999 Data)				
Country	Population (in millions)	Ecological Footprint (acres per person)	Current Capacity (acres per person)	Ecological Deficit (if negative)
World	6,210.1	6.0	4.7	-1.3
Argentina	37.9	7.5	16.5	9.0
Australia	19.7	18.7	36.1	17.4
Austria	8.1	11.7	6.9	-4.8
Bangladesh	134.0	1.3	0.7	-0.6
Brazil	174.5	5.9	14.9	9.0
Canada	31.2	21.8	35.2	13.3
Chile	15.6	7.7	10.5	-2.8
China	1,284.2	3.8	2.6	-1.2
Denmark	5.4	16.2	8.0	-8.2
Egypt	66.2	3.7	1.9	-1.8
Finland	5.2	20.8	21.3	0.5
France	59.3	13.0	7.1	-5.9
Germany	82.2	11.6	4.3	-7.3
India	1,053.4	1.9	1.7	-0.2
Indonesia	217.3	2.8	4.5	1.7
Italy	57.7	9.5	2.9	-6.6
Japan	127.2	11.8	1.7	-10.0
Korea Republic	48.1	8.2	1.8	-6.4
Malaysia	24.4	7.8	8.4	0.6
Mexico	100.8	6.2	4.2	-2.1
Netherlands	16.1	11.9	2.0	-9.9
Norway	4.6	19.6	14.7	-4.9
Pakistan	144.8	1.6	1.0	-0.6
Philippines	78.3	2.9	1.4	-1.5
Poland	38.6	9.1	4.0	-5.1
Russia	144.2	11.1	12.0	0.9
South Africa	44.2	10.7	6.0	-4.7
Spain	39.5	11.5	4.4	-7.1
Sweden	8.9	16.6	18.1	1.5
Switzerland	7.3	10.2	4.5	-5.7
Thailand	61.7	3.8	3.4	-0.4
Turkey	67.2	4.9	3.0	-1.8
United Kingdom	60.2	13.2	4.1	-9.1
United States	288.3	24.0	13.0	-10.9

What does the average footprint in other countries look like? Review some world statistics now to reveal how we, as Americans, compare to other countries.

What can you do to reduce your own ecological footprint? Facilitate a discussion on how we can change our lives to reduce our ecological footprint. Students will get frustrated and say things like, "no one is going to change unless they have to," or "even if I do some of these things, my footprint will still be too high!" Remind students that shrinking your footprint any amount is better than not shrinking it at all. Yes, our problems are overwhelming, but needing 18 acres per person is better than needing 26 acres per person. Positive change, even when smaller than you'd like, is still change for the better! Possible lifestyle changes include:

• Reducing consumerism - remind students that we need to reduce, then reuse, then recycle in that order.

• Explore options to share items in your community. What can you share?

• Avoid items with lot's of packaging, bring your own grocery bags

- Challenge yourself to do with less (something that we learn on a NOLS course).
- Use less energy and water.
- Make lifestyle choices that reduce travel.
- Grow some of your own food.
- Challenge students to explore what activities really enrich their lives. Remind them how much fun they are having just being with other people out here without TV, music, and other commercialized forms of entertainment.

Conclusion
- List three things you want to actively work towards changing in your life to reduce your footprint.
- What does it mean to be in a footprint deficit?
- How can you apply leadership to this concept in your life at home?

Transfer of Learning
Every aspect of this class seeks to help students make wiser choices upon returning home. Control the tone of this class by keeping the tone positive and proactive.

Assessment and Next Steps
Follow-up assignments ideas include having students look at the quiz more closely. Have students determine which categories (food, shelter, mobility, goods) they need to decrease their resource consumption. For each category have them journal about specific changes they could make in their lives. What are the challenges inherent in these changes? How might they encourage and help others make these changes? This is also an ideal time for allowing folks to discuss the ethics behind our resource use. As Americans we consume more resources than any other country. Is that okay? Why or why not? Ideally a follow-up discussion where students share their ideas would allow for collaboration and additional learning. You could weave this journal assignment right into the class by providing a fixed amount of time (20 minutes or so) and then share. I sometimes get students to describe how they want their lives to look in 20 years with respect to resource use (travel, transportation, housing, etc.) If we envision using fewer resources and can still be happy, we're more likely to enact those types of choices.

References
- www.myfootprint.org, and www.footprintnetwork.org

ECOSYSTEM SERVICES – WHAT WE GET BEYOND THE GOODS

This class can be taught independently or integrated into other classes and discussions. The take home message is to remind students that ecosystems provide us with many important things. Many of these things are overlooked, taken for granted, and assumed to be "givens." They are not givens, and as we degrade ecosystems we decrease these services to humanity and other organisms. In the long run this will have a huge cost.

Learning Objectives – The Learner Will Be Able to:
- Explain the difference between ecosystem services and ecosystem goods and provide three examples of each.
- Explain how ecosystem functioning derives ecosystem services and goods.
- Provide examples of human actions that are impacting ecosystem properties, and consequently ecosystem goods & services.
- Understand the link between biodiversity and healthy ecosystem functioning.
- Provide possible "positive steps" for regenerating and maintaining biodiversity to support healthy ecosystems.

What do humans need to survive?
Include as broad a list as possible things beyond the obvious food, shelter, and water. Have students discuss in small groups. Guide them towards identifying food and shelter, and stretching their thoughts to include things like clean water and air. Generate a list on the "board" from their discussions in groups:
- Food
- Shelter (resources that go toward this)
- Water (sometimes free, other times a commodity)
- Moderate weather extremes and their impacts
- Disperse seeds
- Mitigate drought & flood (wetlands)
- Protection from sun's harmful UV rays
- Cycling and storage of nutrients
- Waste detoxification and decomposition
- Control of agricultural pests
- Generate and preserve soils and renew their fertility
- Climate stability
- Clean air and water (wetlands, living organisms, rain)
- Regulation of disease carrying organisms
- Pollination of crops and natural vegetation

Ecosystem Goods and Services
The goods and services we benefit from are a result of the ecological processes and properties of ecosystems all around the world. Ecosystems possess pools of materials (carbon, organic matter, nitrogen, etc.), and ecological processes and cycles (photosynthesis, nitrogen fixation, respiration, organic matter decay, the carbon cycle, the water cycle, etc.) alter these materials in ways that provide the goods and services we need to survive. Most of us understand clearly the goods we receive from ecosystems (those that are bought and sold). We tend to "forget" about all the benefits we derive from ecosystems that are free, however.

Ecosystem Goods – Those resources we obtain from ecosystems that have direct market value (food, medicines, tourism, recreation, genes for biotech, construction materials).

Ecosystem Services – Properties of ecosystems that either directly or indirectly benefit human endeavors (such as climate regulation, clean air & water, soil formation, pollination). These are assigned no value because they're essentially free as long as they exist. Yet without value, many services suffer from the "Tragedy of the Commons."

We currently have no way for assigning economic value to some things even though we must have them to survive. We make attempts with things like pollution credits, carbon credits, etc. Right now there is no cost associated with pollution and degradation of resources. Ecosystem degradation in the long run actually costs money as the goods we can obtain decrease and as we spend money to clean up messes that are health risks or problematic for humans.

Now go back to your comprehensive list and have students determine which of these are assigned economic value and which are not. This defines the difference between ecosystem goods and ecosystem services.

Ecosystem services and goods, taken together, are an indicator of the level of ecosystem functioning. Healthy functioning ecosystems produce ample services and goods in a sustainable manner, whereas degraded ecosystems produce services and goods in a non-renewable manner.

What are ecosystem services worth?

- Flood damage in 1993 in the Mississippi Valley (which no longer has wetlands to absorb additional water) resulted in $12 billion worth of damage.
- 80% of the world's population relies on medicine. Most are derived from plants and animals.
- Over 100,000 species of bats, moths, bees, flies, beetle, birds, and butterflies help pollinate crops with a value estimated at 6 billion annually.
- The approximately 50,000 non-native species in the United States cause major environmental damage and losses totaling approximately $137 Billion per year.

Degradation

Have students brainstorm a list and then fill in ones they may miss.
- Runoff of pesticides, fertilizers, and animals wastes
- Pollution of land, air, and water resources
- Introduction of non-native species
- Overharvesting of fisheries
- Destruction of wetlands
- Erosion of soils
- Deforestation and urban sprawl

Decreased biodiversity is the root cause of degradation of ecosystems. While biodiversity is incredibly complex and it is problematic to link specific decreases in biodiversity to specific ecosystem processes that provide goods and services, there is a clear relationship between decreases in biodiversity and overall ecosystem functioning. It's all the critters that drive biologic processes that provide the goods and services humans rely on. Research is attempting to identify the importance and relationship of specific components of biodiversity with ecosystem properties, goods and services.

Why are humans impacting ecosystem services and goods?

Lead a discussion to derive some ideas before listing these two.
- Growth in scale of human enterprise that damages many of these services (population, per-capita consumption, technology's ability to produce goods for consumption).
- A mismatch between short-term needs and long-term societal well-being.

Conclusion

The take home message of this class is that all things are connected. The choices we make today impact many places and processes on Earth. The results of these impacts ultimately determine the sustainability of Earth's ecosystems and the services they provide to us now and for future generations.

A focus for action is to prevent biodiversity loss, or even better, regenerate biodiversity.

Solutions

What can we do? Facilitate a thorough discussion of things each of us can do to protect biodiversity and our ecosystem services. Discuss the benefits of assigning economic value to these services. Bring up the idea of carbon or pollution credits/penalties. Discuss the downsides to these tactics. Have students journal about this. Provide them with a question or prompt that "jumps" off this topic.

Suggested Journal Prompts

- What choices will you make in your life that will ultimately impact ecosystems and how will you justify those choices?
- How can you alter choices in your life to reduce your impact on earth's systems while still living a fulfilling life?

- Should we assign economic value to ecosystem services? If so, does this ultimately lead to the buying and selling of earth, its organisms, and processes as a commodity resulting in further degradation?
- What should be done about developing nations with large population bases that currently consume few resources per capita but are ramping up to become more like Americans, i.e., India and China?

References

- Nature's Services: Societal Dependence on Natural Ecosystems. Island Press, 1997.
- Hooper, D.U., F.S. Chapin, III, J.J. Ewel, A. Hector, P. Inchausti, S. Lavorel, J.H. Lawton, D.M. Lodge, M. Loreau, S. Naeem, B. Schmid, H. Setala, A.J. Symstad, J. Vandermeer, and D.A. Wardle. (2005). Effects of biodiversity on ecosystem functioning: A consensus of current knowledge. *Ecological Monographs* 75(1): 3-35.
- Pimentel, D, L. Lach, R. Zuniga, and D. Morrison. (2000). Environmental and economic costs of nonindigenous species in the United States. *Bioscience* 50(1): 53-65.

CLIMATE CHANGE

This class serves as a foundation for how to approach the topic of climate change and some of the science that explains why climate changes, how humans are influencing it, and what the impacts of climate change will be. Even if you never teach this as a class, use it as a resource to better educate yourself so that you can weave in these concepts as you travel through your course area.

Learning Objectives – The Learner Will Be Able to:

- Define climate and list three factors that cause climate to fluctuate.
- Explain the influences humans are having on climate.
- Describe some of the more significant worldwide impacts of climate change.
- Speculate as to the local climate changes that might occur and how living communities will change as a result.

Climate defines the average weather patterns over a period of time. factors that influence climate are:
- External factors like shifts in solar intensity and cyclical shifts in earth's orbit. These changes are thought to explain the cyclical ice ages of the past.
- Internal factors like plate tectonics, which reposition continents, shape oceans, and alter landforms like mountains, all affect climate. Increases in CO_2 are thought to exacerbate the greenhouse effect by trapping in heat radiated from the earth causing warming. And, geologic activity like volcanoes, which emit particulate matter, i.e., ash, that reflects some of the sun's energy back to space causing cooling trends.

Human Influences on Climate

- Human influences have increased CO_2 concentrations from 280 ppm in preindustrial times to 387 ppm today mostly from burning fossil fuels.
- Land use changes alter how the earth absorbs and reflects the suns energy and also result in increased CO_2 in the atmosphere as large tracts of forest are burned or cut.
- Aerosols containing sulfates may actually cool temperatures
- Cement manufacturing may represent 5% of the man-made CO_2 released into the atmosphere
- Livestock account for 17% of human produced CO_2 but also release nitrous oxide and methane (both greenhouse gases like CO_2).

- The most significant greenhouse gases that humans are influencing are CO_2 (contributes 9-26%), methane (contributes 4-9%), ozone (contributes 3-7%). Water vapor contributes to the greenhouse effect between 36-70%, yet isn't currently fluctuating as a result of human actions.

Greenhouse Gasses and the Greenhouse effect

The greenhouse effect simply explains how gases in the earth's atmosphere reflect heat back to earth that would otherwise escape into space. Much of the light from the sun penetrates our atmosphere and warms the surface of the planet (land and water). These heated surfaces then radiate heat in the form of infrared light (also known as thermal heat). The more greenhouse gases, the more heat gets trapped in our atmosphere and the warmer things get. Without the greenhouse effect, earth would be completely frozen and life would never have evolved. Our atmosphere traps in heat and keeps things warm enough to support life and, consequently, humans. So the green house effect is good. The question is how are we changing climate and how will those changes interact with other systems (living and non-living). Remember climate always fluctuates, but we may be seeing changes that are very rapid. Rapid changes lead to impacts that disrupt earth's dynamic balance.

How will climate actually change?

- Climate models predict increases in annual global temperature between 0.6° and 4.0° Celsius by the year 2100 (0.6° if greenhouses gases don't increase at all and 4.0° if greenhouse gases continue to rise at their current increasing rates).
- Temperature changes will be greater than averages overland and at higher latitudes (we can expect greater than the average in North America).
- Decreased snow covered areas, increase in thaw depth in permafrost areas, decrease in sea ice extent (including almost no late-summer Arctic ice by 2100 in more severe projections).
- Likely increases in frequency of hot extremes, heat waves and heavy precipitation.
- Likely increases in tropical cyclone intensity, but possibly less total cyclones (scientists are not as confident about this prediction)
- Shifts in typical storm tracks toward the poles.
- Very likely increased precipitation in high latitudes and reduced precipitation in most subtropical land regions.
- High confidence that river runoff will increase in high latitudes and decrease in mid-latitudes (i.e., U.S.) .

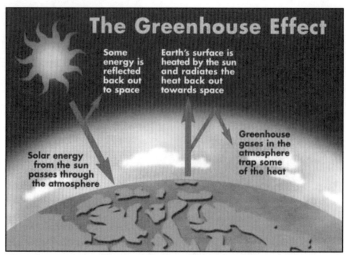

Greenhouse gases such as carbon dioxide released into the atmosphere by human industry are contributing to global climate change through the Greenhouse Gas Effect.

How will climate change impact the earth and humans?

- Water allocation will likely be an issue in many places where precipitation decreases.
- Changes in the frequency and magnitude of weather extremes impact all living systems. The timing of flowering in alpine plants, for instance, is directly tied to snowmelt timing. Some organisms will benefit from changing conditions. Others will not. Many species may shift, through time, to other regions (usually toward the poles and upward in elevation). New communities will form. Many species may no longer compete well for resources in new environments and go locally or globally extinct.
- Human agriculture will likely be impacted differently in different regions.
- Changes in distribution of disease vectors, like mosquitoes, that transmit disease.
- Increased damage from floods and storms.
- Loss of global coastal wetlands.
- Increased wildfire risk in some regions.
- Increased coral bleaching.

What's the climate here?

Define what a climagraph is and help students construct a basic one for your course area. It doesn't have to be correct. But do your

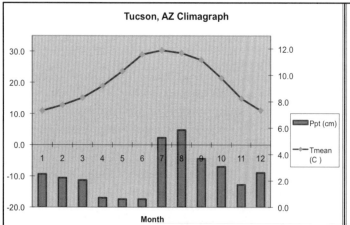

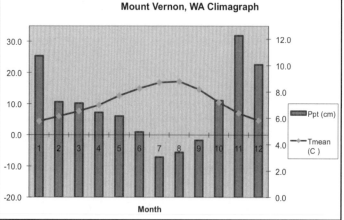

Climagraphs for Tucson Arizona and Mount Vernon Washington—both locations that host NOLS Branches—show average monthly precipitation (bars) in centimeters and average monthly temperature (line) in celsius. Notice that Mt. Vernon has a steadier temperature due to its proximity to the pacific, and that Tucson has a greater temperature fluctuation and less precipitation due to its inland location.

best to estimate the relationship between annual temperature and precipitation by creating two lines that graph annual temperature and precipitation. Does the temperature vary much from summer to winter? What part of the year is it wet and dry? Even if you only come up with descriptors and not a graph, just attempt to help students define the local climate. Use the climagraphs from Tucson (very dry) and Mt. Vernon (very wet) as guides (pg. 64).

Based on what you've learned make some predictions

- How will climate change here (precipitation, temperature, weather extremes, etc.)? Speculation is okay. Try to guide students to some consensus predictions.
- Given these predictions, how will living and non-living systems be impacted? This is a hard question, but an important one. Look at the life forms around you. What limits their existence? Will they benefit from predicted changes? Will they struggle? Will populations likely migrate to other regions? Will rain and snow, or the extremity of weather events be important? How might the landscape look different through time? The important piece here is to attempt to make educated predictions.

Conclusion

- Climate has always changed on planet earth through time. It would change even if we weren't here. However, evidence supports that human influences to earth's systems (predominantly increased concentration of greenhouse gases) are impacting climate.
- Change is neither good nor bad. But change does impact earth: it's processes, systems, and inhabitants (and this includes humans).
- The question for humanity is how will we be impacted? Given the notion that we will likely be impacted significantly, it's in our best interest to slow our influence on climate change and try to mitigate the impacts of those changes.

Transfer of Learning

- Facilitate a discussion on what we can do differently in our day-to-day lives to decrease our contributions to greenhouse gases that are exacerbating climate change. You can likely tie this to the ecological footprint class and environmental ethics class.
- What are some of the positive things that students have seen happening in their homes to address this concern?
- What are some positive social outcomes for society by dealing with this issue?
- See "Educational Problems & Dilemmas: Identifying and Normalizing Value Discussions" in chapter five for some tools to use when presenting this potentially controversial class.

References

- Intergovernmental Panel on Climate Change. 2007. Climate Change Synthesis Report: Summary for Policy Makers, 22 pp.

INVASIVE SPECIES – AGENTS OF CHANGE
By Alexa Callison-Burch

Learning Objectives – The Learner Will Be Able to:

- Consider how invasive species function.
- Understand the degrading effects that invasive species impose.
- Engage in an invasive species discussion from a wilderness expedition perspective.
- Assess the ecological roles particular invasive species play.
- Consider their own responsibility in helping to prevent invasive species distribution and proliferation.

Ask students, what do West Nile virus, rock pigeon invasions, domestic cat proliferation, sudden oak death, whirling disease, Dutch Elm disease, and bird flu all have in common? They are some of the more virulent examples of the thousands of kinds of invasive species. They remain largely unnoticed, but pose a significant threat to our cherished wilderness areas, indigenous ecosystems, and international economies.

Ask for three student volunteers. One student acts as a narrator, the other two as the invasive species actors. Provide the following scenario to interpret on the invasion of the Woody Adelgid (*Adelges tsugae*) - a small, white, beetle looking insect that damages old growth spruce forests and negatively impacts the Christmas tree industry[1]:

- These two are Woody Adelgid larva. Their ancestors were accidentally brought to North America from Asia on trade ships in the nineteenth century. Their family settled in spruce forests in the Sierras and have been wreaking havoc there ever since.
- They were recently transported from California to the Wind River Mountains of Wyoming in the "dirtstickmud schmagma" at the bottom of an unchecked personal student backpack used on a NOLS expedition. There, on night one at camp, they were inadvertently dumped on the ground at the base of a grove of Blue Spruce trees. They hatch, and begin their conquest.
- Immediately they crawl to the new, shooting needles at the end of the branches of the nearest Blue Spruce. There, they begin feasting on phloem sap. While eating, they inject a toxin into the host tree. This toxin kills pine needles and inhibits the plant's vital new growth. Consequently, the tree dies several seasons later.
- Now, with no natural predators, no competing insects, a high dispersal ability, and rapid reproductive rate, the Woody Adelgid flourishes. Soon enough, the tiny insect has killed whole groves of Blue Spruce. The trees that served as a vital component of the Rocky Mountain forest ecosystem are nearly wiped out. And controlling the invasion even more challenging…

Invasive Species and the Problem They Pose

Invasive Species are non-indigenous species imported from foreign ecosystems that adversely affect the native ecosystems they invade, economically and/or environmentally.[1] In the United States alone, the economic costs of nonnative species invasion exceeds $137 billion each year, more than the combined total of all other natural disasters. Most often this manifests in crop destruction. Environmentally, invasive species significantly disrupt delicate ecological webs by outcompeting indigenous species for essential resources. They are the second-most significant threat to native species, behind habitat destruction, imposing on the population decline of nearly half of all endangered species.[2]

Method	Description
Prevention and Containment	This is the single best way to limit impacts from invasive species. Methods include decontamination of freight, packaging materials, and transportation equipment that could contain unknown biotic hitchhikers. (Ask Students: What invasive species exist here in our local wilderness? How did they get here? How can we prevent invasive species proliferation on our NOLS expedition?)
Eradication	Here, early detection and rapid response is an efficient tactic for local eradication of new invaders. Regular monitoring programs to identify new invasive species, in conjunction with any of the control methods listed below, are critical components of this strategy. Systematic early detection programs exist for agricultural pests, but similar programs in wilderness areas are slow to develop, and are underfunded. (Ask Students: What invasive species exist here already? How can we educate ourselves on how to identify them? Further, how can we serve as monitors to help eradicate invasive species here in our wilderness area?)
Control	*Chemical control* (using pesticides, etc.) can effectively kill invasive species, but is expensive and can be problematic on non-target organisms, including humans. *Mechanical control* (physically removing the invasive species or changing habitat conditions) is often successful, but is also expensive and labor intensive. *Biological control* (introducing a natural enemy, i.e., a predator) can be most effective to inhibit invasive species that have established dense populations over large areas. It can be the most environmentally sound method with minimal cost and impact, but controlling the introduced biological agent can be problematic. Sometimes the agent becomes invasive and does additional damage. (Ask Students: What method of control is most appropriate in our Woody Adelgid example? What methods of control can we employ on a NOLS course to eradicate invasive species?)
Restoration	Restoring native communities is an important step to minimize the chances that an area will be re-invaded. Many control techniques inherently create disturbance, which may increase the vulnerability of an area to subsequent invaders. (Ask students: What would restoration look like in our Woody Adelgid example? How might we contribute to native ecosystem restoration on a NOLS course? After our NOLS course?). The reality is that many ecosystems altered by invasive species can never be restored.

This chart highlights five methods for managing invasive species. While solutions exist, they are difficult to implement, costly, and generally yield low success rates.

Who's Responsible

While species can colonize new regions on their own, humans have dramatically increased the magnitude and scale of invasive species' movements. Tens of thousands of invasive species have been introduced in United States alone via human modes. As explorers and stewards of vital wilderness areas on NOLS courses, it is our responsibility to understand the negative impacts invasive species impose and make conscientious efforts to prevent their proliferation. Further, inhibiting species invasion is a conscientious global responsibility of all citizens.

The Ecology of Invasive Species

Not all species transported to a new place become "invasive." Only those with adaptations that allow them to successfully compete for limited resources will displace native organisms (ecological interactions include competition and parasitism). Many transplanted species would simply die out, unable to access and compete for resources in a new environment. Faced with new and aggressively competitive invasive species, native species are caught off guard lacking suitable adaptations in a newly competitive environment. Their niche has changed. They either die out, or, through successive generations, develop adaptations that allow them to compete. On a small scale, an invasive species acts as a changing variable that can exceed an ecosystem's tolerances in which it maintained a dynamic balance. This results in an ecosystem collapse, and ultimately a new and different ecosystem with a different dynamic balance. There are always winners and losers.

Solutions

Prepare and present the table on the next page for students illustrating ways to control invasive species. Check for student understanding in the guided questions listed at the end of each method. The instructors might also encourage independent student reflection on invasive species by asking students to respond to these questions in a journal writing assignment:

Conclusion and Transfer of Learning

Invasive species significantly disrupt delicate native ecosystems, usually by out competing indigenous species for vital resources. Human trafficking of invasives has primarily caused their global proliferation. Maintaining native ecosystems free of invasive species is a critical piece in sustaining a biologically diverse, healthy planet. In many ways, this is already a global, irreversible pandemic. While the damage done may be a result of human actions, change is inevitable. Invasive species are not evil. They are just playing their role in new environments. The irony is that thousands of years from now, what we now call invasive species will be native species. They may one day be outcompeted by other species that get transported. What we must face is that our spread of invasive species across the planet will have a profound impact on ecosystems and ultimately a profound impact on humanity. It is everyone's responsibility to try to prevent invasive species from proliferating further.

On NOLS courses, we can begin by assessing the modes in which we might transport invasive species into the wilderness areas we explore. Further, we can help eradicate invasive species by learning how to detect and report them to appropriate agencies. Finally, in good stewardship, we might begin by taking time to help remove invasive species from wildernesses we cherish.

References
[2]Ecological Society of America - "Invasion". www.esa.org/education/edup-dfs/invasion.pdf

ENVIRONMENTAL ISSUE DEBATE FORMAT
Adapted From Classes By – Marco Johnson and Ashley Graves Lanfer

Learning Objectives – The Learner Will Be Able to:
- Explain an environmental issue and state what is at stake
- Explain multiple perspectives related to the issue
- Propose possible solutions to the issue
- Form a personal opinion on how they think the issue should be approached

Choose some environmental or land management issue that is relevant to the course area you are visiting as a debate topic. The following are some suggestions:

Resource Extraction Issues
- Gas & oil developments/drilling – economic, social, air/water quality, habitat
- Logging – economic, social, air/water quality, habitat
- Mining – economic, social, air/water quality, habitat
- Renewable energy development vs. non-renewable energy development

Development Issues
- Habitat destruction as a result of some proposed development (parks, facilities)

Land Management Issues
- Grazing impacts on range, water quality, air quality
- Water allocation for ranching, farming, recreation & native species habitat (fish)
- Motorized vs. non-motorized recreation (winter & summer)
- Fixed anchor use in wilderness areas

Environmental Issues
- Wildfire management (suppression vs. let it burn)
- Invasive species management – poisons, trapping, challenges, impact of vehicles and other recreation on seed dispersal
- Endangered species – who's responsible for loss of value when habitat is protected?
- Impacts of climate change on ecosystems – pine bark beetles, caribou.

Procedure
The pubic policy site on Rendezvous has "Fact Sheets" for most course areas that can be helpful.
- Divide students into groups representing one viewpoint. Give them a handout that details the issue and "their group's viewpoint" either a day in advance or just in advance of the debate. Either way, provide adequate time for students to review the information before the debate so they come with information fresh in their minds.
- Explain that you expect every student to chime in at some point with his or her thoughts. Follow through at the end with students who may have been silent and ask them to share their own thoughts on the issue given the debate.

- Choose one students to act as an unbiased moderator during the debate.
- Each group should prepare an argument that takes no more than 10-15 minutes to present. Then after each group delivers their argument, give each group 5 minutes to rebut.

Caveat
While we may think we are "preaching to the choir" when discussing issues with students and other instructors, we may find that our viewpoints differ more than we anticipated. Avoid going into the debate assuming your opinion is the "best" opinion.

Conclusion
Allow 15 minutes to conclude and debrief the debate with some of the following questions or activities:
- What were the facts, assumptions, and values from each argument? These are often confused during debates and lead to confusion on issues. Good arguments are based on sound facts, not assumptions and values, although values may guide what actions to take as a result on interpreting certain facts.

FACTS	• Public lands are used for both logging and recreation. • We all use wood products • Different logging methods have different impacts.
ASSUMPTIONS	• Americans want to protect more land from logging. • Hiking is less destructive than logging. • People who hike are more responsible stewards of the Earth than people who log.
VALUES	• It is good to protect land. • It is better to enjoy the land and leave it unchanged than to use the land.

Follow-up Questions
- Which questions were answered?
- Which questions remain unanswered?
- Did anyone change his or her opinion?
- Do people have a greater awareness of the different sides of the issue?

Transfer of Learning
What might you do differently in your day-to-day lives as a result of a better understanding of this issue? Our decisions and actions do impact these issues. We can differ what we consume, alter our lifestyles, participate in decision-making processes (EA comments, call representatives, vote).

Assessment and Next Steps
- Participation can be used for assessment as long as you are clear about that in advance.
- A follow-up journal reflection related to the debate could also be used as an assessment. Focus the reflection on some transference piece.

WOOD FIRES VERSUS GAS STOVES— AN ECOLOGICAL PERSPECTIVE

By John Gookin, PhD

Purpose

This discussion aims to shorten the feedback cycle for energy use and help students think in whole systems.

Lesson plan

Many of us backpacker-types intuitively associate cooking on wood as causing *more* impact than cooking on a gas stove: the information below busts that myth. Here we consider the full life cycles of wood and gasoline, and look at the impacts from the perspective of the biosphere.

- Timing: This topic is a good 15-minute diversion while baking, especially when using either twiggy fires or coals from a campfire.

Learning Objectives—The Learner Will Be Able to:

- Understand the concept of carbon neutrality.
- Understand the concept of carbon sequestration.
- Acquire some direct experience with their own impact regarding energy use.
- Practice fuel self-sufficiency.
- Display the ability to judge wood availability, camper density, and other factors related to whether fires are ecologically appropriate.
- (Optional) understand some basic values and logistics of biomass power plants.
- (Optional) apply the concept of wedges.

Outline

Carbon neutral means that the activity has a net zero carbon footprint. Review the carbon cycle, photosynthesis, respiration, & carbon sequestration. Run through examples from the large-scale to the small-scale.

- Power plants: biomass vs. fossil fuels
- Cars: alcohol vs. gasoline
- Cooking: wood vs. gasoline

Use the Socratic method to guide a listing of the pros and cons of cooking on wood and gas.

- Global impact: Carbon neutrality
- Local impact
- Convenience: Perception that cooking on gas is faster than cooking on wood.
- Pack weight: Total weights of stoves and fuels

Background Notes

There are some new stoves being built for backpackers that use "carbon neutral" fuels. Carbon neutral means that during the life cycle of the fuel, it emits as much CO_2 into the atmosphere as it absorbs. NOLS has played with a few of these stoves on lightweight courses, not because they are green, but because they are lightweight stove systems.

Fossil fuels are our current fuel standard at NOLS. They not only put 100% of their carbon into the atmosphere, but they add an extra 25% for the energy it takes to drill, pump, refine, and distribute the fuel. This means they are -25% carbon neutral. Burning fossil fuels takes dense carbon chains (oil) from underground, combusts them, and sends their CO_2 byproduct into our atmosphere and oceans. Fossil fuels came from the atmosphere millions of years ago, but they are currently *sequestered* (tied up) deep in the earth. Burning fossil fuels is one of the leading causes of climate change. Since CO_2

makes water acidic, CO_2 in clouds contributes to one of the big environmental threats to mountain ecosystems: acid rain. Carbon neutral fuels like alcohol and wood avoid feeding this carbon cycle.

Alcohol comes from biological breakdown (fermentation) of plants: it *could* be a carbon neutral fuel, but unfortunately fossil fuels are used to make alcohol commercially. Using corn-based alcohol mixed with gasoline to make E85 automotive fuel (85% alcohol) was a great idea, but in reality it has limited environmental benefits because of fossil fuel consumption related to planting, fertilizing, and harvesting the corn, and the heavy use of more fossil fuels in the alcohol fermentation and distillation processes. Alcohol stoves are sometimes lighter than gasoline stoves but, like E85 gas, they are only 15-30% carbon neutral. Using more organic practices for raising and processing corn (or other biomass) quickly doubles the carbon neutrality of alcohol.

Wood is often the only 100% carbon neutral fuel we can use. This is because the wood is synthesized via photosynthesis from atmospheric CO_2, providing a carbon neutral effect over the life of the tree. The twig burning *Sierra zip stove* has been around for decades. The *Woodgas Stove* burns wood so efficiently that it boils water as quickly as an MSR stove, and remarkably it doesn't even get your pots dirty. The *Bush Buddy* is a favorite of some NOLS "light and fast" instructors because, unlike the other two stoves, it doesn't need AA batteries to run a fan. The *Littlbug* is probably the lightest and simplest of these stoves and it can burn either wood or alcohol, making it versatile in mixed terrain. These stoves, and the MacGuyver-esque hobo stoves, made from tin cans (check them out on Youtube), make it easier to cook on wood, and lab tests show they use half as much wood and burn it more cleanly than using an open campfire. But efficiency aside, even open campfires and twiggy fires are systematically "greener" for the biosphere than any of the fossil fuel burning stoves.

Some circumstances make carbon neutral fuels very convenient. Sometimes it's convenient while fishing with a group of students to cook trout in an existing fire ring. This is especially efficient if fishing on a long day-hike. Wood is an excellent backup fuel in case your expedition runs out of naptha (gas). I (JG) did a 30-day sea kayak expedition in Belize in 1983 with no stove, cooking on coconut husks and driftwood, just as the locals did. I did learn to carry some high quality tinder to get fires going during wet conditions, and I carried a machete, which helped me split driftwood for tinder during our monsoon week. I have had students in Canyonlands gather dry cow dung so they could make tea during their solos. These systems took more time than cooking on gas stoves, but they were extremely convenient in the situations, and they were free from dependence on the industrial logistics supply chain we habitually take for granted.

I am not advocating that we switch our whole logistics machine and start cooking exclusively on wood (as we used to), however I think NOLS instructors should know the ecological merits of baking using wood fires. Rather than apologizing for causing the impact of cooking on wood, we should be celebrating that we are cooking on wood rather than oil. There are also huge issues on the horizon that make the related knowledge and attitudes transferable to commercial power plants (below). In summary, here are some pros and cons of cooking on local wood fuel.

Pros: Wood is a renewable and carbon neutral resource. Wood is abundant in most NOLS operating areas. Fire is a natural changing force in the ecology of many forests. The air pollution from burning a handful of wood is insignificant compared to the pollution from naturally occurring forest fires. When NOLS courses cooked exclusively on wood in the 1960's, campers carried small bundles of twigs to have some good starter wood: this weighs a lot less than a stove and fuel bottles full of white gas.

Cons: Fires are illegal in some areas and under certain conditions. Burning wood causes more *local* impact than burning white gas (*naptha*) brought from oil wells. These impacts can include denuding trees, smoke, and accidental man-made forest fires. This can compromise the wilderness compared to importing our fuels. Burning wood usually takes more time to cook than by burning naptha. Open fires burn inefficiently so they tend to get soot on pots (which is why pots and pans used to live in *pot bags* at NOLS). Using local wood for fuel is only appropriate in healthy highly productive forests, or in tree die-off areas. High use areas like campgrounds may not tolerate any additional harvesting of wood, so you might need to haul your wood a long way. Lighting fires can be tough in some environmental conditions.

One educational opportunity of cooking on local fuels is that it gets people in direct contact with their own impact. It literally shortens the feedback loop for our consumption of energy. We should be able to guide this new awareness of personal impact without a huge guilt trip. It is okay that we eat, drink, poop, breathe, and do other bodily functions that cause ecological impacts. This sounds so elementary to be potentially insulting to students, but most of us are protected from the direct experience of our own day-to-day impacts because our food seems to originate from big stores, our poop goes away down toilets, and energy is available by flicking a switch. Becoming more aware of our impacts, and owning them, is an important step in becoming a responsible steward and citizen (see the *ecological footprint* exercise in this book for more on this). This awareness needs to be up front and personal, not just a theoretical discussion.

Power Plants

There are many initiatives to shift power generation in the USA towards more renewable resources. One is called *Repower America*. Based on Al Gore's proposal, it looks at the holistic system of renewable generation, energy efficiency, smarter distribution systems, and plug-in cars. Using the sustainability education model, changes like these happen by gradual replacement, not by replacing yesterday's technology all at once.

One type of renewable power generation being looked at is burning wood. Problems include getting the wood pieces small enough to mix with air and burn efficiently, transportation of this low density fuel, collocation of natural timber waste products and power plants, and balancing environmental impacts with economic values. Life Cycle Assessments (LCA) that address these costs and benefits show very different biomass generation models for diverse places like California, Oregon, Wisconsin, and Texas. These LCA models also generally show that right now, biomass is a more expensive fuel than natural gas. Economics is not the only factor in these decisions, but it is a huge factor. This is why forestry labs across the US are looking at more economical ways to generate power with biomass. Like wind energy, there may be some consumer driven initiatives that insist on greener power mixes. These consumer initiatives sometimes tip the scales in getting some renewable energy products off the ground. Then, once novel renewable power systems come online, feedback systems help us learn a lot more about using the new technology more practically.

Small-scale biomass power plants are already available. These allow farms, sawmills, and other industries to burn their natural biological waste products and turn the energy into electricity used on-site. In many cases this keeps bio-waste out of landfills or prevents burning of bio-wastes in the fields. These power plants have their own air pollution concerns, just like any other type of power plant, but they are carbon neutral and have many added efficiencies for small industries.

Sitting around a campfire, passing around the brownies just baked on that fire, might be an excellent time to discuss our energy future because we would be modeling exactly what we were discussing about using more and more renewable resources for our energy needs. We wouldn't just be talking about wedges, we would *be the wedge*.

References

- Biomass Cooking Stoves   http://bioenergylists.org/en
- Bush Buddy Stove   http://www.bushbuddy.ca/index1.html
- Littlbug Stove   http://www.littlbug.com/stove.html
- National Renewable Energy Laboratory/ Biomass Research http://www.nrel.gov/biomass/
- Repower America   http://www.repoweramerica.org/plan/
- Sierra Zip Stove http://www.zzstove.com/
- Small scale biomass fueled gas turbine power plant www.epa.gov/ap-pcdwww/apb/bioen98.pdf
- USFS Wood Energy Lab   http://www.fpl.fs.fed.us/tmu/wood_for_energy/basicenergyinformation.html
- Woodgas stove   http://woodgas-stove.com/content/Comparison.html

CHAPTER SEVEN: TRANSFER OF LEARNING

INTEGRATING TRANSFER OF LEARNING

By Jamie O'Donnell and Pat Kearney

A NOLS experience has value in and of itself. First and foremost, a NOLS course should be a significant life experience, and it usually is (Kellert, 1998). But our mission and educational outcomes ultimately seek to benefit students after they leave NOLS. Our alumni say that transfer of learning happens at NOLS. They say that NOLS helped them develop a personal perspective that life can be simpler, an appreciation for nature, a desire to be outdoors, ability to function under difficult conditions, ability to manage conflict, and ability to make informed and thoughtful decisions, among 19 significant factors that NOLS alumni say is critical in their lives and they attribute to developing at NOLS (Sibthorp, 2008). Alums from one to ten years report the same transfer, showing that these are the lessons that survived the usual barrier of reentry into the home social environment.

Some courses promote more transfer of learning than others. When alumni were asked what it was about NOLS that supported the learning that transferred to their lives, they reported that the NOLS lessons they retained were relevant to them, they saw good role modeling, they valued the locations they visited, and they had ample opportunities to practice things (Sibthorp, 2011). Many of these transfer mechanisms were related to instructor behaviors. Peak experiences were key to learning, but the leadership classes that preceded the peak experience made the experiences especially successful and memorable.

To support transfer of learning, we must thoughtfully engage students in experiences that they can transfer or connect to other aspects of their lives. While students may not recognize how the experiences, skills and knowledge they gain during a course can and will benefit their lives, we can increase the potential for transfer by helping them make important connections during their course. In this way, we make an experience relevant during the course, and provide examples for how learning can be applied once they return home.

Environmental studies curriculum represents a valuable opportunity for NOLS to influence students' lives after NOLS. For many students, their NOLS experience represents the first extended period of time they have spent in wilderness. This experience, combined with knowledge of ecology and the natural sciences stands to influence their value system as well as their ethics. An understanding of how public lands are run and the challenges inherent in managing these lands for different uses can lead to further learning throughout their lives. Yet, how we choose to frame their NOLS experience impacts the number and strength of connections students make between their NOLS experience and other aspects of their lives. Throughout the entire course—not just towards the end—we must thoughtfully and actively design our environmental studies curriculum to this end.

Much of what we hope for our students' transfer of environmental studies relates very closely to our leadership curriculum. We not only want our students to feel personal growth from a NOLS wilderness experience, but we want them to act on what they learn. This requires a step-by-step approach beginning with assessing self. A genuine self-assessment helps each of us to identify where we are versus where we hope to go (self-awareness, judgment and decision making). Once we define goals and understand what we need to do to reach them, we may begin the process of changing our behaviors (competence, vision and action, tolerance for adversity and uncertainty). Once we've applied change to our own lives we can begin leading others in similar endeavors (communication, expedition behavior). The following diagram details that process.

While transfer of learning is depicted as the last step in the ES curriculum model, it should be infused throughout the curriculum. Each class, activity, and discussion should be connected to aspects of life after NOLS. This not only helps demonstrate how something can be transferred for students, but also provides a "place" for new information to be "stored" in our student's brain, increasing the chances they'll remember it. As an example, when we teach students how to poop in the woods, we can discuss some of the ecology that determines how and why we choose a particular method. We can also introduce the idea of nutrient cycles. At this point we can reference the ways in which these same principles are applied to solid waste disposal in municipal waste treatment plants or even in our gardens and compost bins at home. In this way, new information about how we dispose of waste in the wilderness is connected to the science (how and why) and to decision-making back at home.

A significant challenge at NOLS is helping students to transfer the knowledge they learn in the wilderness setting to the non-wilderness setting. It is relatively easy for students to transfer the technical skills they learn into other environments (for example shelter

---

ASSESS SELF
- Learn about:
  - The interaction of living and non-living systems
  - Public lands management and policy
  - Relevant environmental issues
- Define your environmental ethic
- Assess your behaviors:
  - Ecological footprint
  - Reflection

CHANGE SELF
- Significant life experience supports development of identity
- Apply knowledge to decision-making
- Narrow the gap between your environmental values and your behaviors
- Engage as a continuing learner and steward of the environment

LEAD OTHERS
- Help teach others important knowledge
- Share passion and wilderness experiences with others
- Role model responsible environmental behavior
- Assume leadership roles in education and policy positions

set-up). There are many reasons why these skills transfers well, it is a task repeated many times throughout a course, there are only a few new necessary things to learn to transfer (appropriate environmental anchors, etc.) and significantly, the context (being outside), remains constant. For learning interpersonal skills and values (environment science, leadership, etc.) to transfer to the very different contexts between the wilderness and home environments we need to actively encourage reflective learning. That means asking students to reflect on their learning, highlight learning and encourage critical thinking throughout the course. Metacognition, or an awareness of thinking, can also help learning to transfer. Some ways to infuse this into courses and classes are: deliberate pauses to reflect during an experience, problem solving in pairs, having students actively teach each other, taking time to draw connections/dissimilarities between topics and to debrief.

A study published in 1995 by Hammitt et. al. revealed that NOLS courses do influence students,' "responsible environmental behaviors (REB)." However, surveys conducted four months after course completion indicated that REB decreased as students tended to revert back to their pre-course position as they were distanced from their NOLS experience. Our challenge is to help students make this connection and then maintain it despite the pressures that exist in our day-to-day lives. Methods these researchers suggested to help achieve this goal are to revisit transfer at the end of course. Remind, revisit, and reconnect. We should remind our students about what they learned. We should revisit the notion that we lived simply during the course with very few "creature comforts," yet lived well. Hammitt et. al. also suggests that reconnecting with students after their course would help prevent students from distancing themselves from their NOLS experience. Having students write a letter to themselves that the branch mails one year after a course could be a good way to remind students of how they felt during their course. A student journaling activity about their environmental values and ethics (See Chapter Five: Ethics) provides an opportunity for reflection. This activity could be framed as a letter to self that details how students hope to be enacting their own personal ethic in a year's time.

Ideas for Increasing Transfer of Learning

- Ecological footprinting represents an important tool for assessing one's resource use. This activity directly transfers the concept of sustainability to life after NOLS as it allows students to assess their resource use and then analyze what lifestyle choices require the greatest amount of energy and/or land. The strength in the activity lies first in assessing one's resource consumption and then in discussing alternative choices that would reduce these impacts.
- The journal prompt on "Defining Your Own Environmental Ethic" is a great tool for challenging students to define how they hope to behave with respect to the environment in the future. First they must explore what they value and then how those values define their ethic. Challenge students to depict what their lives will look like in five years or ten years in terms of energy use, consumption, transportation, career, community participation, food, etc.
- Writing a personal letter to self, sent later as a way for students to reconnect with their experience and thoughts when back in their home environment.
- Final night discussion about what they learned, what they hope for the future, what challenges they anticipate and specifically what they hope to transfer.
- The four R's: Remind, Revisit, Reflect and Reconnect.

References

- Hammit, J. P., Freimund, W., Watson, A., Brod, R., & Monz, C. (1995). *Responsible environmental behavior: Metaphoric transference of minimum-impact ideology*: National Outdoor Leadership School (NOLS).
- Kellert, S. (1998). *A national study of outdoor wilderness experience*. Yale School Of Forestry.
- Sibthorp J., Furman, N., Paisley, K., Gookin, J. & Schumann, S. (2011). *Mechanisms of learning transfer in adventure education: Qualitative results from the NOLS transfer survey. Journal of Experiential Education*.
- Sibthorp, J., Paisley, K., Furman, N., Schumann, S., & Gookin, J. (2008). Long-term impacts attributed to participation in wilderness education: preliminary findings from NOLS. *Research in Outdoor Education, 2008*.

THE CHALLENGE OF CHANGE:

Want to dig deeper? Lead a class on the challenges of creating true change. This page gives more insight into NOLS' work, struggles, and successes with implementing environmentally sustainable operating practices.

NOLS TRANSPORTATION

What and why?
NOLS vehicles emit 40 percent of NOLS' carbon footprint. We start with efficiency: carpooling, minimizing deadhead runs and idling, being diligent with maintenance practices and disposing of transportation waste properly. We're also trying out green technologies: hybrids, ethanol, biodiesel, and compressed natural gas.

Does it work?
Yes: carpooling and being efficient with vehicle use reduced our emissions. We also had success with ethanol and hybrid vehicles. Sort of: We are still trying other technologies, sorting out the challenges, and grappling with the various environmental concerns of each of them.

What we learned.
Start small. If it works, go big. If it doesn't work, no harm done.

Discussion: Could NOLS operate without fossil fuel vehicles (don't forget air travel)? Could you? How do different geographical locations support or discourage different types of transportation (for example, is riding your bike easier in an urban or rural environment)?

NOLS FRONTCOUNTRY

What and why?
NOLS facilities are responsible for 45 percent of NOLS' carbon footprint. Our first step is to be more efficient and then move to alternate products. Producing our own renewable energy lowers our carbon footprint and increases our educational opportunities.

Does it work?
Yes: insulation, efficient appliances, and alternative energy installations all reduce our carbon footprint. Environmentally preferable purchasing standards decrease the use of unfriendly materials. No: Comfort, cost, and convenience often clash with efforts to use less energy, and purchase fewer and different products.

What we learned.
Behavioral change is hard, and it takes time.

Discussion: Is it more important to generate alternative energy or use energy more efficiently? Why?

THE FIELD

What and why?
Just like the frontcountry, what we do here impacts the quality of our environment and life. In the backcountry we practice Leave No Trace ethics, such as disposing of waste properly and traveling and camping on durable surfaces, to minimize our impact.

Does it work?
Pretty well! There's always room for improvement, and we continuously work with our students to do better. Compared to our frontcountry impact, though, we're doing great in the field.

What we learned.
Practicing an ethic, no matter how small the practice is, is valuable. High expectations are inspiring.

Discussion: What Leave No Trace habits are you forming? Which of these habits can you practice in the front country? How do they transfer?

HOME

Tell us about your challenges and successes with low-impact practices at home.

What and why?

Does it work?

What you learned.

Discussion: Are there sustainable opportunities that are available to some but not others? Are these opportunities dictated by geography? Socioeconomic status? Other factors?